"With wisdom and warmth, Court[...] [...]ders through an overview of the Bible. S[...] [...]:heo-logical insights with engaging stories in a way that makes this resource beneficial to women who have walked with the Lord for years, as well as those new to the faith. If you want to understand the story of the Bible, then *From Garden to Glory* is for you."

—**Melissa Kruger**, author and vice president of The Gospel Coalition

"*From Garden to Glory* is a wonderful invitation to trace—and be changed by!—the overarching story of the Bible from beginning to end. Whether you're a new believer or a seasoned saint, this book will encourage your walk with Christ."

—**Ruth Chou Simons**, *Wall Street Journal* bestselling author, artist, and founder of GraceLaced

"If you've ever wished that you could understand the big picture of the Bible, this resource will help you know how to do it! Based on a solid grasp of the Bible and theology, and full of practical illustrations, *From Garden to Glory* will walk you through the overarching story that runs from one end of the Bible to the other. It will help you to know the Bible better and give you a greater understanding of God, his glorious purpose for his world, and how your life relates to that purpose. It is both helpful and hopeful, and those who go through it will reap rich rewards!"

—**Jay Sklar**, Professor of Old Testament, Covenant Theological Seminary

"*From Garden to Glory* will help you better understand the Bible's story so that you might know and love the Author behind every word. As she nestles us in God's story of redemption, Courtney lovingly encourages us to treasure and live out its truths. This is an incredibly helpful resource that I will reference and recommend regularly."

—**Hunter Beless**, founder of Journeywomen Ministries; author of *Read it, See it, Say it, Sing it!* and *Amy Carmichael: The Brown-Eyed Girl Who Learned to Pray*

FROM GARDEN

to GLORY

COURTNEY DOCTOR

HARVEST HOUSE PUBLISHERS
EUGENE, OREGON

Published in association with the literary agency of Wolgemuth & Wilson.

Cover design by by Faceout Studio, Spencer Fuller
Cover photo by © pear.art, Valery Rybakow / Shutterstock
Interior design by Aesthetic Soup

For bulk, special sales, or ministry purchases, please call 1-800-547-8979.
Email: CustomerService@hhpbooks.com

From Garden to Glory

Copyright © 2024 by Courtney Doctor
Published by Harvest House Publishers
Eugene, Oregon 97408
www.harvesthousepublishers.com

ISBN 978-0-7369-8834-6 (pbk)
ISBN 978-0-7369-8835-3 (eBook)

Library of Congress Control Number: 2023945086

Printed in the United States of America

24 25 26 27 28 29 30 31 32 / BP / 10 9 8 7 6 5 4 3 2 1

For my mom, Mary Ellen Randall.
You have shown me how to keep my eyes
on the big picture and trust the One who holds the
whole story together from beginning to end.
I love you.

*"The LORD is good; his steadfast love endures forever,
and his faithfulness to all generations."*

—PSALM 100:5

ACKNOWLEDGMENTS

This book was originally written as a study that was published in 2016. I had wanted to write that study ever since my first class at Covenant Theological Seminary in the fall of 2010—Covenant Theology. Five professors—Drs. C.J. (Jack) Collins, Brad Matthews, Greg Perry, Jay Sklar, and Michael Williams—took turns showing us the beauty and coherency of the biblical story. My debt of gratitude begins with those men, but it extends to all of my professors, who taught me how to use what I learned in that first class.

There have been many friends and co-laborers along the way who have offered support and encouragement in extraordinary ways, but none more than Bunny Hathaway. Your expertise, sharp eyes, and many hours resulted in more beauty and clarity. You have been a true source of joy and encouragement in this journey. I owe a tremendous debt of gratitude to the ladies at the Kirk of the Hills Tuesday morning Bible study—your willingness to bear with, pray for, and encourage me during this writing project was a true help and blessing.

Stephen Estock, Karen Hodge, and the whole team at CDM, thank you for your willingness and kindness in first publishing the study. You have prayed for the study and for me. You have encouraged, supported, and helped in so many ways, and I will always be grateful to have partnered with you in the first phase of this project.

I'm indebted to Bob Hawkins and the entire team at Harvest House for your willingness to see this study turn into a book! It's been a joy to work with you, and I look forward to our partnership in the gospel.

With the deepest gratitude, I want to thank every person who has used this material as a study (some of you multiple times!). So many of you have reached out with encouragement and kindness that has meant so much. I hope this book continues to serve you well.

Last, but hardly least, I want to thank my family. I am so grateful for each of you and all the wonderful ways you love so well. My cup overflows!

Now to him who is able to do far more abundantly than all that we ask or think, according to the power at work within us, to him be glory in the church and in Christ Jesus throughout all generations, forever and ever. Amen.

EPHESIANS 3:20-21

CONTENTS

FOREWORD
NANCY GUTHRIE

The collective voice of the world around us and the instinctual voice inside us teaches us to think and say, "My life is about me—who I am, what I will do, what I will accomplish and become." We think this is empowering and freeing. But it can also be defeating. The truth is, we are limited. Our lives are fragile. We fail. So it is actually very good news that our lives are not defined by our own accomplishments or failures, by what we've made happen or what has happened to us, by what we've consumed or what has consumed us. The good news of gospel is that if we are joined to Christ, our lives are defined by who Christ is, by what Christ has accomplished, and is yet to accomplish in the future. It is his story that gives meaning and purpose and hope to our stories. This means that we really need to know his story. We need to understand how his story has developed to this point in history, where we are in the story, and what is yet to come. That is what *From Garden to Glory* does for us. It brings together our bits of Bible knowledge into a cohesive storyline that helps us make sense of the Bible and make sense of our lives.

In this book, Courtney Doctor ably grounds our understanding of what this beautiful and yet broken world is all about in what happened in the Garden of Eden. It anchors our understanding of our need for salvation in the salvation of Israel out of slavery in Egypt. It feeds our hope of living in a world under a just government and righteous ruler in God's gift of a king. It explains our longing for a future and a home and relationship in the future home and the relationship God set out to restore to his people after they forfeited that home and relationship in the first garden. This ancient story answers some of the most significant questions in our lives. It explains what we were made for and therefore why we feel so much joy when we're fulfilling that purpose. It also explains why we experience so much pain, frustration, and sorrow in this life even as it sets our hope on a day in the future when that pain, frustration, and sorrow will be a thing of the past.

Every good story has a crisis. And the crisis in this story is the impact of Adam's sin on all of humanity. Every good story also comes to a climax. And, oh, what an incredible climax the story of the Bible comes to in the life, death, and resurrection of Jesus Christ! In *From Garden to Glory*, we get more than a vague sense of what that means as Courtney pulls back the curtain of the simple phrase "Jesus saves," enabling us to see the way Jesus saves in specifics. We see what it means for us that he is the Second Adam. We see how in his death and resurrection he reconciled us to God, redeemed us from slavery to sin, offered himself as the once-for-all sacrifice for sin and overcame the serpent and his evil.

Seeing what Jesus did to accomplish our salvation in his first coming increases our love for him. And catching a glimpse of how he will bring us into the fullness of that salvation when he comes again makes us long for him! We say, "Come quickly, Lord Jesus!"

This is a story that resolves into glory—the glory we long for, the glory we were made for. I hope you will take in the wonder of the story Courtney so helpfully articulates on the pages to come. May it saturate your thinking about your own story so that you will more clearly see what it means that you have been united to him by faith. May it increase your longing for the glory to come.

In anticipation of the greater garden and the unending glory to come.

—*Nancy Guthrie*

WHY THIS BOOK?

For many of us, the Bible is a somewhat mysterious book. I look back and realize that, as a child, I was fairly superstitious about it. I owned a small, white leather Bible with a zippered cover. My grandmother brought it to me from Israel, which only added to its mystery. I put it on a special shelf, by itself, and I certainly never put other books on top of it! I rarely took it off that shelf; but when I did, I would ceremoniously open it and hope somehow the "magic" verse would appear before me. I had great reverence for the Bible, but no love of it. I suspected it held deep mysteries and even treasures, although I had no idea what it was about. But what I now know is that God has given us his Word not to *be* a mystery, but to *reveal* mystery.

God is mysterious, but he has given us his Word to reveal himself—make himself known—to us. He does not merely make a list of his attributes in order that we would know *about* him (i.e., I am holy, eternal, powerful, good, loving, etc.). Instead, he recorded a story that both tells us who he is and shows us what he is like. For example, he tells us he is "merciful and gracious, slow to anger, and abounding in steadfast love" (Exodus 34:6), and then he shows us throughout the story that he is merciful, gracious, loving, and slow to anger with the rebellious Israelites—and ultimately, with us—by sending Jesus! The whole Bible is a story about God, and it has been given to us so that we can know him—not just about him, but know him personally.

The Bible is a book that is meant to be read, understood, loved, and applied. As we learn about God, we also learn about us. We learn who we are, who we were created to be, and how we are to live. We learn that God is holy and we are not; we learn that he is omnipotent and we are dependent; we learn that he is the redeemer and we are the ones who need to be redeemed. And we learn that, because we are created in his image and are meant to multiply that image throughout the world, we have meaning, purpose, and significance. As we read this story, we are learning not just about God, but about ourselves, our purpose, and even our final destiny.

But when it comes to reading the Bible, it's not always easy to know where to start. If we're not supposed to just open the Bible and hope the perfect verse will appear before our eyes, then how should we approach it? My hope is that this book will help us answer that question. This is an overview of the whole story the Bible tells—a story that begins in a garden and ends in glory. It is a 30,000-foot view of the grand sweep of redemption. We are going to "fly over" the story in such a way that we can look at it in its entirety, from beginning to end.

Every chapter has a Scripture passage for you to memorize. There is a page at the end of the book on which you'll have the opportunity to write each passage from memory. Memorizing these verses will help you to hide God's Word in your heart, and enable you to remember and more easily share God's redemptive story with others.

As we look at the story from this 30,000-foot perspective, I pray four things will happen. First, that the Bible will become less mysterious and more loved as we learn to read it as the story it is. The individual parts will make sense only when they are read in light of the entire story. Second, that your hunger for the Word of God will grow as you discover how amazing and brilliant this story is. We will see how it began, how it ends, and how the pieces in between fit together. I hope that you will experience a spark that ignites a passion for studying God's Word, as well as gain a tool that will equip you in that study. Third, I pray that you will come to a greater understanding of your own value and significance as you come to a deeper appreciation of how your life is wrapped up in this story. The Author invites you to know this great story, enter into it, and share it with others because this story is your story too. This story is meant to change your story. And fourth, I pray that the God of the Bible—Father, Son, and Holy Spirit— will be exalted, proclaimed, and worshipped because of our time together in his Word.

YOUR INVITATION TO JOIN THE GREATEST DRAMA OF ALL TIME

If you've seen *The Passion of the Christ*, you know that it evokes strong emotions. This movie tells the story of the brutal 24 hours surrounding Jesus's crucifixion. When it was first released, most people were so moved by the depiction of Christ's sufferings that they left the theater either in silence or tears—or both. Some said that they didn't (or couldn't) talk to anyone until the next day.

But not everyone felt that way. One young man, when interviewed and asked about his reaction to the movie, reflected sincerely and said, "I guess it was okay, but it didn't have much of a plot." That might strike some of us as funny at first, and as tragic once we let his comment sink in. But he has a point.

If you grew up in the church or went to Sunday school as a child, when you saw *The Passion*, you sat down in the theater knowing the movie was picking up a storyline that was already underway. You knew most of the back story. But for this young man, it was like going to see *Tangled* (Disney's version of the Rapunzel story) and only viewing the part where Rapunzel was rescued from the tower. If you didn't know why she was in the tower in the first place or what was going to happen to her now that she was out, your understanding would be diminished. Or it would be like watching *The Lord of the Rings* and only seeing the scene where Frodo and Sam struggle up the mountain and throw the ring into the pit of fire. Surely, you would wonder why the struggle was so difficult and why disposing of the ring was so necessary.

Maybe you didn't grow up hearing what Paul Harvey called "the rest of the story," and, like the young moviegoer, wonder what difference the horrible and gruesome death of a man on a cross more than 2,000 years ago could possibly make to you. Well, if that is the case, have I got a story for you!

But for those of us who did grow up hearing the backstory, before we either chuckle or roll our eyes at this young man, we need to stop and think about how, so often, we explain our Christian faith to others in a way that perpetuates this truncated version of the story. If you are like me, you have probably been taught to share your faith by explaining, "Jesus died on the cross to forgive us of our sins and take us to live with him in heaven for all eternity." And that is true. But it's far from all! We are living in the middle of the greatest drama of all time, and the Bible is the recording of how this great story began—as well as how it will end.

Herman Bavinck, a Dutch theologian in the 1800s, summed it up this way: "The essence of the Christian religion is this, that the creation of the Father, devastated by sin, is restored in the death of the Son of God, and re-created by the Holy Spirit into the kingdom of God."[1] Do you see what Bavinck did? He started with creation and ended with the consummated kingdom of God; he started in the garden and ended in glory. He was saying that this great story involves God the Father, God the Son, and God the Holy Spirit. He showed that the original creation was very good, and the final re-creation will be very, very good—but that something, namely sin, has devastated that good creation. We can see that something had to happen in order to rescue and restore that original good creation. And that is the story of redemption—God working through real events and real people for the salvation of his people!

Before we begin, let me offer a word of warning: Please don't think that by calling this a story that I mean it's not true. Sometimes the word *story* is used to refer to something that is made up or make-believe. Sometimes it is used to mean a lie (Did you just tell a story?). But *story* can also be used to mean an accurate account of something that happened (Have I told you the story of our crazy summer vacation?). It is in this last sense that I call the grand drama of redemption a story—not just *a* story, but *the* story, the one in which our very lives are anchored. However, don't for a minute think that you can just sit back and enjoy the show. This drama invites you in, calls you onto the stage, and transforms you into one of its innumerable participants. So, without further ado, let the lights dim and the curtain go up. Get ready for the greatest drama of all time.

CHAPTER 1

CLIFFSNOTES

Scripture Memory

"No prophecy was ever produced by the will of man, but men spoke from God as they were carried along by the Holy Spirit" (2 Peter 1:21).

Pray

"Call to me and I will answer you, and will tell you
great and hidden things that you have not known"
(Jeremiah 33:3). Father, open my heart and eyes to the
wonders of your Word and the glories of your work.

When I was growing up, family vacations were great. But the process of getting out the door to begin the vacation was not great. Usually, my brother and I were hyped up, eager to leave. My dad was focused on the goal: Get everyone in the car and get on the road. My mom was running around making sure the coffee pot was off, the windows were locked, the vacuum was put away, and the pillows were straight. Eventually the moment came when all of us were finally in the car and ready to go! Or so we thought. Inevitably, before we left the driveway, my dad would stop and look at the map (this was long before GPS) one more time to make sure he knew exactly where we were headed.

This first chapter is somewhat like that. You are here, ready to get going. But before we "hit the road" (in chapter 2), we are going to stop and make sure we are properly oriented. We need to "look at the map" before we head out.

When you were in high school, did you use CliffsNotes (those handy little summaries of literary works written for students) to help you pass an English class? If you were like me, you used them for all the wrong reasons—mainly so you wouldn't have to actually read the assigned book. But just because we might have used them wrongly does not mean they didn't have a helpful purpose.

CliffsNotes are written to help provide a framework for understanding a book. CliffsNotes usually start with some fundamental elements—information about the author, the setting, the genre, major themes, and purpose of the book—and then they break down the individual chapters. That is how we are going to start this study. Chapter 1 is like reading a CliffsNotes guide for the Bible. We are going to consider the Author (and authors), the setting, the genre, the plot summaries, and the purpose of the Bible so that we have a framework to help us better understand the story the Bible tells.

AUTHOR(S)

Have you ever had times when, as you read a book, you felt as though you could almost hear the author's voice? Or maybe you've had that happen when you received a note from a dear friend. As you read the note, you could almost hear the writer's voice.

When I read a book, if I don't know the author personally, I like to know something about them. If I'm reading a book on theology, I like to know what the author believes, or maybe a little bit about his or her life. Knowing something about an author informs how we read their work.

The same is true for the Bible. But this can be a little tricky because when we talk about the author of Scripture, we can mean the divine Author (God), or the men who captured the words on the page (Moses, David, Paul, Peter, etc.). As the living Word of God, the Bible is different from any other book we read. It's not just the work of a human being or even a group of humans. The Bible was inspired by God (meaning God himself spoke the words). We read in 2 Timothy 3:16 that "all Scripture is breathed out by God." But it was written down by numerous men over the course of more than 1,000 years. In 2 Peter 1:21, Peter wrote, "No prophecy was ever produced by the will of man, but men spoke from God as they were carried along by the Holy Spirit."

These men, however, were doing more than mindlessly transcribing the words of God. Part of the miracle and the mystery of the Bible is that God used ordinary men—their individual personalities, unique life experiences, and different cultures—to capture his very thoughts and words. God has always allowed his people to participate in his purposes.

As we are sitting in our imaginary driveway orienting ourselves for this journey, this is a foundational truth we must know. It will shape our understanding of exactly what we are reading, how we are to read it, and how we are to respond. As Moses said, these are not mere words for us; they are our very life (Deuteronomy 32:47). And why is that? Because they are the very words of God himself!

One of the most comforting truths about knowing that God is the divine Author of every word in Scripture is stated in Isaiah 46:9-10, where God said, "I am God, and there is no other; I am God, and there is none like me, declaring the end from the beginning and from ancient times things not yet done, saying, 'My counsel shall stand, and I will accomplish all my purpose.'"

Only the author of a story can know where the story is headed before he starts writing. It is the will and intent of the author that carries a story forward from beginning to end. The Author of this marvelous book is on his throne on every page and in every moment of every day. God knows where the story is headed, and he will accomplish all his purposes. This is true not just of the overall story of redemption (God knew the end before he began), but it is also true of our individual lives. He is weaving together a grand story of redemption for all his children, and he is weaving together a grand story of his grace for you. God knows where your story is headed, and he intends to work all things together for your good (Romans 8:28-39) as only a divine author could.

SETTING

I have a friend who is an archaeologist. He is like a modern-day Indiana Jones and has spent considerable time in different parts of the world digging for artifacts. If he were to find a Roman coin as he was digging, what factors would affect the conclusions he could draw about that coin?

For starters, his geographical location would matter. A Roman coin found in Egypt is going to mean something different than a Roman coin found in Texas. Also, the layer of his dig would matter. If he were to find the coin in a layer where everything around it was from the 1800s, his conclusions would be different than if he had found the coin in a layer from the first century. The geographical setting of his find will inform his understanding of it.

The historical reality also matters. If my friend were to say he had found the remains of a unicorn, what would you think? Most of us would say, "Wait a minute. A unicorn?" We would think that he had lost his mind! Why? Because we know that unicorns are mythological, and in an archaeological dig, he should only find things that were/are real. An archaeologist can only dig up the remains of things that actually existed in a certain place at a certain time. So historical reality is also a key to his findings.

Like my friend on his digs, several things are important to us as we study to understand God and his Word. One is the historical reality of the Bible—God works in real people, in real places, in real times—real settings! As Michael Williams once stated in a class I attended, "The biblical authors…knew that faith without real world, historical fact, is not faith but mere superstition."[1]

This is important to keep in mind because we need to know that God's revelation to us is grounded in events that actually happened! We are able to be saved because a real man was really born, really died, and really rose again. Paul reminded us of this when he said, "If Christ has not been raised, then our preaching is in vain and your faith is in vain" (1 Corinthians 15:14). Paul was saying that if the crucifixion and resurrection had not really happened to a real man (Jesus) at a very real moment in time (circa AD 33) in a real location (outside the city of Jerusalem), then our faith is pointless. That makes the historical setting of the Bible a big deal!

If we don't take some time to anchor the story of "God's works in our world" in settings of real time and real places, then we're left with reading the Bible as a collection of moralistic stories that may or may not have happened. Or as mythology that does nothing more than display the consequences of both good and bad behavior. In such unanchored stories, God and his actions on our behalf can become like that unicorn—a fun idea, but nothing we need to take too seriously. But, praise God, the events in the Bible actually took place in locations that we can visit. This means that when we read the Bible, we are not merely reading good ideas about how we should live, we are reading about a living God acting and working for his people. And that very same God continues to act and work for his people in our very real world today.

In the introduction, I said that the story of redemption could be summarized as God working through real events and real people for the salvation of his people. The God who created everything does not stand far off and throw moralistic ideas at us; instead, he engages with and steps into his creation—he works for us in real time and space!

As you read through Scripture, you'll see that God goes out of his way to let his readers know that what he is telling them is no mythical tale. He gives us dates, names, and facts that anchor his Word in historical settings. Think about how God had Moses begin the book of Deuteronomy:

> These are the words that Moses spoke to all Israel beyond the Jordan in the wilderness, in the Arabah opposite Suph, between Paran and Tophel, Laban, Hazeroth, and Dizahab. It is eleven days' journey from Horeb by the way of Mount Seir to Kadesh-barnea. In the fortieth year, on the first day of the eleventh month, Moses spoke to the people of Israel according to all that the LORD had given him in commandment to them, after he had defeated Sihon the king of the Amorites, who lived in Heshbon, and Og the king of Bashan, who lived in Ashtaroth and in Edrei (1:1-4).

Look at all the details that give us the historical setting. Exact locations, exact dates, and references to other historical events. This is how God makes sure we know that this story is historically grounded. Ezekiel begins with, "In the thirtieth year, in the fourth month, on the fifth day of the month, as I was among the exiles by the Chebar canal, the heavens were opened, and I saw visions of God" (verse 1). God made sure we were oriented both geographically and temporally before he gave us, through Ezekiel, the grand visions that he gave.

When you read the Bible and come to sections that give many very specific details, ask yourself why those details are included. God wants us to know that what he has recorded for us really happened. That's why, in Luke's Gospel, before we read about the birth of Jesus, we read, "In those days a decree went out from Caesar Augustus that all the world should be registered. This was the first registration when Quirinius was governor of Syria" (2:1-2).

We need to know that God works through and amid human events; the miraculous occurs amid the mundane, both then and now.

GENRE

If you have read Tolkien's *The Lord of the Rings*, I doubt you were frustrated with him because you couldn't find Middle-earth on Google maps. You probably even reacted in fear when Shelob (a giant spider) was about to eat Frodo (a hobbit)—even though you knew that neither of these beings actually existed. Why? Because you knew what genre you were reading. *The Lord of the Rings* is not a history book; it is a made-up story of mythical and magical characters who delight and capture our imaginations. Knowing what you are reading is an important part of knowing how to read it.

But is the Bible like *The Lord of the Rings*—a fantasy? No! We've already observed that what is given to us in Scripture is a record of real events, real people, and a real God speaking, acting, and moving in real time and real places.

So what genre is Scripture? That's not an easy question to answer because the Bible contains different genres. The psalms are poetry, the New Testament contains personal letters (epistles), and the proverbs are, well...proverbs. But does that mean the Bible is made up of a bunch of fragmented and maybe even unrelated parts? No!

The overarching genre of Scripture, the genre that holds it all together as one, coherent piece of literature, is narrative. The Bible is a story—not a fictional story, but a story nonetheless—one story, written over many centuries. Within that story we find historical records (e.g., 1 and 2 Chronicles), poetry (e.g., Psalms), historical narrative (e.g., Exodus), and several other forms of literature, but the overarching genre is narrative.

One of my favorite books, *A Severe Mercy* by Sheldon Vanauken, is an autobiographical narrative account of the author's marriage. Within the story, the author shares letters that he received from his dear friend, C.S. Lewis. When I get to those letters, I'm not confused even though the genre has shifted. I understand that I am to read the letters within the storyline. And the letters make greater sense within the even greater story being told.

The same is true for us as we encounter different genres within the big storyline of the Bible. They make the most sense when we read them as part of the whole. Paul's letters are not random, stand-alone documents. Rather, they are letters found within a bigger story—and they make the most sense within that story. David's psalms are not arbitrary songs. They contribute to the story being told.

God could have simply documented the facts: that he made everything good, we broke it, and now he is fixing it again. But he didn't. Like I mentioned in the introduction, God doesn't just *tell* us about himself; he *shows* us who he is through what he does in the story. Let me say that again: God doesn't just tell us about himself; he shows us who he is through what he does. He both tells us he is faithful and shows us his faithfulness through stories about men and women he forgave, promises he fulfilled, and plans he brought to fruition.

Stories are powerful. We are all moved more by a good story than by a list of facts meant only to inform us. By using narrative, God shows us that his main goal is not to merely inform us, but to transform us and invite us into his story. We are not to know him solely in an intellectual way, but in a relational way—and, as a result, we are to love him with all our hearts, minds, souls, and strength. The story helps us do that.

As we study this great story of redemption, my prayer is that we will see how the stories of our lives are part of God's bigger story. You and your life are anything but insignificant—you are part of something grand and glorious! As we see how the story continues from one generation to the next, from one person to the next, and from one place to the next, so will we see how it continues to include you and me today.

> You and your life are anything but insignificant—you are part of something grand and glorious!

PLOT SUMMARIES

Did your English teacher ever make you write plot summaries? Mine did, and I was horrible at this. I had such a hard time deciding which details should be included. What events in the plot were crucial? What events weren't? But, without fail, whenever I did the work of writing a summary, I ended up understanding the story better. Writing a summary meant I had to know the main plot and be able to trace how the author accomplished his or her purpose through the development of the plot. By the time I was done, I found that I was better able to explain what the book was about.

If someone were to ask you "What is the Bible about?" what would you tell them? "Jesus" is always a good answer, but what would that mean to someone who doesn't know anything about him? Remember the man I told you about in the introduction—the one who thought *The Passion* didn't have much of a plot? What could you tell him that would help him to see the events portrayed in the movie were part of a much bigger story? The movie portrays the high point of the story, but it is not a summary of the whole story. The movie chronicles a week in time, but that week was the culmination of thousands of years of promises and expectations.

Likewise, the ongoing effects of that one week have changed the course of history for all time—including our lives today. If we were asked to write a summary of the story, we would not begin with a baby in a manger. We would have to start in Genesis 1 because, like in most stories, the first few chapters of a book contain key information, like the setting, the characters, and even the conflict.

At the end of this chapter, I will ask you to take a minute to write down what you think might be some of the major events in the storyline of Scripture. I will ask you to do this again at the end of the book, and give you the opportunity to compare your two answers. But for now, pick a few events in the Bible and consider whether they might be crucial events in the storyline. If the story begins with God making all things good, what might be the next major event?

The Bible itself gives us multiple plot summaries that help us to see which events the Author considers key moments. And it is important to know the key moments not only so we can summarize the story of Scripture for our own comprehension and for the comprehension of others, but so we will know all that God has done, and respond faithfully.

In Joshua 24, God reminded the people, through Joshua, of

their collective story thus far. Pay attention to what God considered to be key moments as well as what he wanted their response to be:

> Joshua gathered all the tribes of Israel to Shechem and summoned the elders, the heads, the judges, and the officers of Israel. And they presented themselves before God. And Joshua said to all the people, "Thus says the LORD, the God of Israel, 'Long ago, your fathers lived beyond the Euphrates, Terah, the father of Abraham and of Nahor; and they served other gods. Then I took your father Abraham from beyond the River and led him through all the land of Canaan, and made his offspring many. I gave him Isaac. And to Isaac I gave Jacob and Esau. And I gave Esau the hill country of Seir to possess, but Jacob and his children went down to Egypt. And I sent Moses and Aaron, and I plagued Egypt with what I did in the midst of it, and afterward I brought you out.

> "'Then I brought your fathers out of Egypt, and you came to the sea. And the Egyptians pursued your fathers with chariots and horsemen to the Red Sea. And when they cried to the LORD, he put darkness between you and the Egyptians and made the sea come upon them and cover them; and your eyes saw what I did in Egypt. And you lived in the wilderness a long time. Then I brought you to the land of the Amorites, who lived on the other side of the Jordan. They fought with you, and I gave them into your hand, and you took possession of their land, and I destroyed them before you. Then Balak the son of Zippor, king of Moab, arose and fought against Israel. And he sent and invited Balaam the son of Beor to curse you, but I would not listen to

Balaam. Indeed, he blessed you. So I delivered you out
of his hand. And you went over the Jordan and came
to Jericho, and the leaders of Jericho fought against
you, and also the Amorites, the Perizzites, the Canaan-
ites, the Hittites, the Girgashites, the Hivites, and the
Jebusites. And I gave them into your hand. And I sent
the hornet before you, which drove them out before
you, the two kings of the Amorites; it was not by your
sword or by your bow. I gave you a land on which you
had not labored and cities that you had not built, and
you dwell in them. You eat the fruit of vineyards and
olive orchards that you did not plant.'

"Now therefore fear the LORD and serve him in sincerity and in faithfulness. Put away the gods that your
fathers served beyond the River and in Egypt, and serve
the LORD."

Did you see the response God wanted from his people because
of all he had done? We will be talking more about this in other
chapters, but it truly does matter how we respond to God and
all he has done.

One of my hopes is that, by the time you have finished this
book, you will be better able to summarize and articulate what
this story is about. As we better understand what the key events in
the storyline are, we, like Moses, Joshua, and Luke, will be better
able to not only respond faithfully, but also be able to tell others
about our God and his glorious plan of salvation.

AUTHOR'S PURPOSE

When my husband Craig and I started dating, he lived in Col-
orado, and I was in Oklahoma. This was before cell phones, and
our phone bills were sky-high! But we were in love, and what is

money when you are in love? We would talk for hours, just getting to know each other. Craig loves to tell the story about being on the phone with me one night while he was standing in the hallway, and his friends passed him to go out for the evening. They teased him about not going with them. He just smiled and stayed on the phone. But when they came back to the fraternity house many hours later and we were *still* on the phone, they about fell over laughing at him! He has not heard the end of that one.

During this time, I would write long letters telling Craig about me, my days, my life. We were getting to know each other. But I had to decide what to tell him and what not to tell him. If I had kept something hidden, Craig would not have known about it. He could know me only to the extent that I was willing to reveal myself to him. But we were so eager to know each other, we readily shared a lot about ourselves—our hopes, dreams, fears, thoughts, aspirations—anything that would help the other to know us better. We wanted to know and be known.

The Bible is how God has chosen to reveal himself to us. The only reason we know anything about God is because he wants us to know him. We do not discover God; God reveals himself to us. He has chosen to make himself known to us! Has he told us everything there is to know about him? Absolutely not! But as Peter tells us in 2 Peter 1:3, "His divine power has granted to us *all things* that pertain to life and godliness, through the knowledge of him who called us to his own glory and excellence" (emphasis added). God has told us everything that we need to know; he has told us both who he is and what he has done. But not all revelation is the same.

Scripture tells us that the heavens and earth reveal God's existence, power, and glory. Psalm 19:1 states, "The heavens declare the glory of God, and the sky above proclaims his handiwork." Psalm 50:6 says, "The heavens declare his righteousness," and Romans

1:19-20 tells us, "What can be known about God is plain to them, because God has shown it to them. For his invisible attributes, namely, his eternal power and divine nature, have been clearly perceived, ever since the creation of the world, in the things that have been made. So they are without excuse." This is called God's general revelation. He reveals himself in a general way to everyone who has ever lived.

But is that all the revelation we need? Does God's general revelation provide enough information for us to know "all things that pertain to life and godliness"? No. Although there are people who seem to think so. They say that they don't need church or the Bible; they can simply "worship God in nature." One of the reasons God's general revelation of himself is not enough for us is because we don't understand or accurately interpret this revelation. As Michael Williams has said, "Sin has chewed the wires to the radio. God is still broadcasting, but we don't hear clearly."[2] We need help to understand what God has revealed!

Thankfully, God has not only revealed himself generally, but he has also revealed himself specifically. The Bible is part of God's specific revelation to us. And part of what God does as he reveals himself to us in Scripture is explain what we see but don't understand. That is why merely observing nature is not enough. We need the Author of all creation to comment on his work. There is a reason that the word *author* is the root of *authority*—the one who originated the idea has the most authority to explain the idea. We need God to explain his revelation to us. But there is even more we need.

In John 17:3, Jesus said, "This is eternal life, that they know you, the only true God, and Jesus Christ whom you have sent." Knowing things about God is wonderful, but salvation is found not in knowing about him, but in knowing him personally through his ultimate revelation—his Son, Jesus. God has revealed himself fully in his Son, Jesus. Jesus himself said, "Whoever has seen me has seen the Father" (John 14:9), and we are told in Colossians 1:15 that "He [Jesus] is the image of the invisible God."

God has chosen to reveal himself to us so that we will know him. But knowledge of him is not the end goal. The reason God has revealed himself is for our salvation and his worship. General revelation reveals that God exists, and specific revelation reveals how we can be saved. We must respond to what God

> God has recorded this great story of all he has done not simply so that we will know about him, but so that we will know him, believe him, be saved by him, and worship him forever.

has told us about himself. He has recorded this great story of all he has done not simply so that we will know about him, but so that we will know him, believe him, be saved by him, and worship him forever.

Points to Remember from Chapter 1

- God is the ultimate Author of Scripture—the one who knows the end from the beginning.

- The events of Scripture are anchored in history—real time, real places, real people.

- The Bible is a narrative account of God and his work in our world, in which he tells us and shows us who he is.

- The story is still unfolding, which means we get to be a part of it!

- God, the Author of our story, has chosen to reveal himself because he wants us to know him!

- God reveals himself through his creation but even more fully through his Word—both the written Word and the Word who took on flesh and dwelled among us.

Discussion Questions

1. Read Acts 4:24-25. Whose "mouth" was used? Who was the one using the "mouth"? What is the name of the man who penned this verse?

2. Read Acts 3:15 and Hebrews 12:2 ("founder" can also be translated "author"). Of what else is God the Author?

3. In what ways does the thought that God, the Author of your story, knows the end before he ever begins change the way you view your current circumstances, challenges, suffering, and trials?

4. Read Luke 2:1-5. What do you learn about the setting (time and place)? How is this an example of the miraculous occurring in the midst of the mundane?

5. Think about the very real circumstances in your life today—the joys and the struggles. God works in real people, in real time, and in real places—today just like in AD 33. How is God working in the mundane and difficult places in your life?

6. Read 2 Samuel 12:1-7. How does God use a story to reveal truth as well as invite a response in David's life?

7. Read 1 John 5:11-12. Where is eternal life found?

8. Read John 17:3. What knowledge is needed for eternal life?

9. Either write below or share with your group one point, truth, or lesson that either challenged or encouraged you from this chapter.

For Further Study

1. Read Acts 9:1-9. Why is the historical setting (reality) of this scene important? What is miraculous, and what is mundane?

2. Read the summaries in Nehemiah 9:6-37 and Psalm 105. What events are recorded in both passages, and what are mentioned only in Nehemiah? What are some possible reasons for that?

3. Read Revelation 22:18-19. What does this tell us about the revelation of God through his written Word?

4. Read Philippians 2:9-11. What will the final response of every person be?

5. Take some time to write a summary of the Bible—write down what you think might be some of the major events in the storyline of Scripture. You will have the opportunity to do this again when you finish this book, at which time you will compare your two answers.

CHAPTER 2

ONCE UPON A TIME

Scripture Memory

"God saw everything that he had made, and behold, it was very good. And there was evening and there was morning, the sixth day" (Genesis 1:31).

Pray

"The grass withers, the flower fades, but the word of our God will stand forever" (Isaiah 40:8). Father, help me to see more of your greatness and to live more in your grace.

I hope you won't judge me, but I love all the Disney princess movies. Every single one. But in my house, because my two oldest children are sons, our family tended to watch more man movies than chick flicks. If you don't know the difference, my husband offers this clarification: Man movies are about a lot of people dying quickly, and chick flicks are about one person dying slowly. He may be right, but in this book, I'm not talking about chick flicks or man movies. I am talking about a story that all of us—men and women, old and young—gravitate to. You know what I'm talking about: a story of danger and rescue, love and passion, heroes and villains, and of great evil being triumphed over by even greater good.

My high school English teacher taught me that all good stories have at least four main parts: introduction, conflict, climax, and conclusion. The introduction makes the reader aware of the characters and setting. The conflict moves the story forward; it is the main problem that will need to be resolved. The climax of the story is the spectacular solution to the problem. And the conclusion wraps up the story in a way that brings resolution.

Think of every fairy tale you've ever watched. What storyline did they follow? Most start with "Once upon a time," and the music is sweet, the birds are singing, and the sun is shining. All of a sudden, the music changes and an evil witch comes on the scene. At this point the great conflict is revealed. Before too long, however, to our great relief, the trumpets blare and the knight in shining armor rides in for the rescue. There is a great battle, an even greater victory, and the story ends with the music again playing sweetly, the birds singing once again, and the sun shining brighter than it did before. At the end, we gladly hear, "They all lived happily ever after." Our hearts leap at this good news. We gravitate toward this type of story over and over because we know this story—it's our story. Instead of "Once upon a time… but then an evil witch…the knight in shining armor…and happily ever after," the four parts of our story are typically called creation, fall, redemption, and new creation.

I love the movie *Tangled*, which, as I mentioned in the introduction, is Disney's version of the Rapunzel story. It is a story of rescue and romance, love and laughter, danger and dancing. What could be better? But let's look closely at the beginning of the story. Within the first two minutes, we learn some crucial parts of the story (and if we were in line getting popcorn and we missed that part, then the rest of movie didn't make as much sense). Flynn Rider, the soon-to-be-hero, opens the movie with a line that informs the audience of two facts: His death will be an integral part of the story, but somehow, all will be okay in the end. After that line, the story flashes back to a previous time and we're shown a magical flower that has the power to heal the wounded and sick. With these first lines and the opening scene, the audience learns that there is an origin or source of that which is good—the magic flower—and that this goodness will be able to overcome the bad. The audience is given hope. The scene then skips to a shot of a glorious kingdom on a beautiful island, ruled by a good and loving king and queen. In two minutes, what have we learned? The setting for the entire story.

In a much more grand and glorious way, Genesis 1–2 is the introduction for our story. In these two chapters, we learn what the world was supposed to be like—and, if we miss these chapters, the rest of the story just doesn't make as much sense. It is at the beginning that we get a glimpse into the time when all was as it should be.

THE KINGDOM

At the beginning of any good fairy tale, how is the kingdom usually portrayed? As mentioned above, the sun is usually shining, birds are singing, and there is joy and laughter in the air. Why? Because the author wants the audience to know what the world looked like when all was good and right. There is a way that the world is "supposed to be." By showing this, we can more clearly see the devastation any disruption causes—and understand why we spend the rest of the story longing for conditions to be returned to the way they were.

Think of *The Lion King*. How did it begin? With a magnificent sunrise, beautiful views of animals roaming, and the order of creation functioning properly. But what happened when Scar (the evil brother) became king? The land became dry and barren, there was not enough food or water, and animals languished and died. The kingdom was affected by the virtue of the king, and the beauty of the kingdom as seen in the movie's introduction serves to highlight the severity of the devastation that takes place after the disruption.

Our story is no fairy tale, yet God began his story with a beautiful glimpse of what life was supposed to be like in his kingdom: there was love, beauty, order, and peace. And this initial glimpse in Genesis chapters 1 and 2 is a snapshot of what the kingdom of God was meant to look like. We are not supposed to view these chapters simply as a description of what had happened in the past, but as a window into the delight and love our Father has for his creation.

One of the amazing facts about this kingdom is that it was intended to be the perfect home not only for the King, but for his subjects as well. The goodness of the kingdom was one of the ways God showed his goodness to us. God lavished Adam and Eve with his "very good" creation, and it is in this goodness that we were intended to live.

The Garden of Eden is a picture of what life looks like when the kingdom of God is in full effect without the disruption of sin. As the story progresses, we will see that God is in the business of restoring his kingdom. And just wait until we get to the end of the story—the final kingdom is even more glorious than the first!

THE KING

The kingdom, as it was intended, would have been a magnificent place. All was good—very good. But a kingdom is only as good as its king. It is the king who determines whether peace rules and people flourish. He is the one who maintains the goodness of the kingdom.

When we think of a king or monarch, most of us probably think of things like ruler, power, and responsibility. And all of these are true. But there is one aspect of kingship that is crucial to our understanding: It is the aspect of sovereign decree—when a king speaks, his words become law. Because kings have supreme authority, their words are expected to be obeyed, immediately.

When we read Genesis 1, we observe that everything obeyed God. Repeatedly when God spoke, we read, "And it was so." Every atom, every molecule, every particle obeyed the voice of the true King.

In Genesis 1–2, God is not explicitly called the King. With that in mind, it's important to consider the different ways authors let their readers know about the characters in their stories. Some authors tell you about the characters in direct ways. For example, in *Tangled*, the author has Flynn Rider overtly say that "the king and queen are loved." But other authors will describe their characters through what they do. A character's actions help the reader to infer certain information about that character.

Think of *Mary Poppins*. The author never explicitly tells us that Mary is some sort of magical being. But he shows us in numerous different ways. To start with, Mary uses an umbrella to fly onto the scene. Then she opens her carpet bag and proceeds to pull out a large lamp, a mirror, and a coat rack—all objects that are entirely too large to fit into her bag. She talks with animals and rides a carousel horse off through the countryside. The reader is clearly supposed to pick up on what the author is trying to show—that Mary is no ordinary person.

In no way am I equating God with Mary Poppins. Rather, I am merely pointing out the different ways an author can provide the information he wants the reader to have. In our story, Moses (the author of Genesis) does not tell us that God is the King—but he absolutely shows us that God is the great King over all things. He does this by describing what God does and what happens as a result.

Knowing that God is the high King of heaven is important to our understanding of what happened in Genesis 3, the great rebellion. When Adam and Eve rebelled, they did so against the one true King of heaven and earth. And the rest of the story is about God, the one true King, bringing his people back to live under his good rule and reign. We will look at this theme as the story progresses and will greatly rejoice to see its glorious conclusion!

But before we go any further, we must stop and talk about the very first audience of Genesis 1–2. In order to read anything well, we must first understand what the author wanted his original audience to know. People have strong opinions about Genesis 1–2. There are debates about when creation occurred, how long it took God to create everything, the length of a "day," and, of course, what happened to the dinosaurs. So it is helpful to step back and remind ourselves who the first audience of Genesis was and what the author was conveying to them—not just to interpret Scripture well, but to apply it well too!

Moses wrote the first five books of the Bible, and the first people to read these books were the newly delivered Hebrew people. God had just brought them out of Egypt from slavery (we'll be talking a lot more about them in the chapters to come). They had been born as slaves and had been oppressed, afflicted, and vulnerable to Pharaoh's every whim. Pharaoh was a cruel taskmaster who held absolute power in Egypt.

Now, imagine you are standing on the other side of the Red Sea. That king, Pharaoh, the one who seemed so powerful, that one who had held the lives of your children in his hands, has been destroyed and you have been delivered. You are no longer a slave! Wouldn't you want to know who it was that was more powerful than Pharaoh? Read all of Genesis 1 through the lens of being a newly rescued, former slave. God is being portrayed not just as a king, but as *the* King! And part of the good news of Genesis 1–2 is that God is not only the high King of heaven and earth, powerful, majestic, and sovereign. He is also a most loving Father.

THE LOVE OF A GOOD FATHER

On any given Father's Day, many posts on social media give tribute to either to a person's father, or to the father of a person's own children. It is a day filled with all the positive things you can say about a father. Some thank their dad for providing for them, others thank their dad for loving them and for "always being there" when they needed advice or a hug. It is a sweet day to think about all that a dad is supposed to be.

However, not everyone has or had a good dad. We don't live in the "once upon a time" anymore, and our world is not the way it's supposed to be. And one of the realities of living between "once upon a time" and "happily ever after" is that dads don't always function the way they should.

Not all dads are kind or trustworthy, not all dads are faithful or stick around, and not all dads provide what their children need. Some dads are harsh, absent, drunkards, or abusive. We live in an age filled with deadbeat dads, and everyone—believers and unbelievers alike—seems to know that it is not right to have a child and not care for that child. Our government will even legally punish a father who does not help and care for his children. When dads don't function as they should, the impact on us is tremendous because we know, deep down inside, that things are supposed to be different. Fathers should be truly good—they are supposed to provide for, protect, love, engage with, know, spend time with, and delight in their children.

Sadly, many people believe God is like a deadbeat dad—that he simply created the world, stepped out of the picture, and now sits back and lets things play out without his involvement. They assume he is not involved in the care of his children because he is either disinterested or unwilling. But Scripture tells us a completely different story.

When we consider who God is as Father, we must realize he is not like imperfect, earthly fathers. Rather, he is the kind of Father we were created to have. So no matter where your earthly father falls on the scale of fatherhood—from someone who is your hero to someone who failed or even hurt you—your heavenly Father is perfect in his love in every possible way. He is safe. He is kind. He is faithful. And he is the only one who can truly satisfy the deepest longing of your heart to be perfectly loved.

> Your heavenly Father is perfect in his love in every possible way. He is...the only one who can truly satisfy the deepest longing of your heart to be perfectly loved.

As we think about what it means that God is our Father, let's look at four specific aspects of fatherhood: presence, provision, protection, and parameters. Obviously, there is more to parenting than these four aspects, but these four are key. We want our fathers to be present with us, to spend time with us, and to know us. We need them to provide for us. And we long for their protection and need them to set parameters for us—to teach us what is good and what is not. God does all these things when he cares for his children.

Presence: In Genesis 3, after Adam and Eve sinned, we read, "They heard the sound of the Lord God walking in the garden in the cool of the day, and the man and his wife hid themselves from the presence of the LORD God among the trees of the garden. But the LORD God called to the man and said to him, 'Where are you?'" (verses 8-9). What I want us to see is this: If Adam and Eve chose to hide from the presence of the Lord, then in Eden, they experienced the presence of the Lord! God himself walked with them and they talked with him. God was present with his children; he spent time with them; he knew them, loved them, and communicated with them.

Provision, Protection, and Parameters: These three aspects are intimately intertwined. Just as the parameters I set for my children are for their protection (don't run into the street), so are the parameters that God sets—and his provisions are within the boundary of his parameters.

We see in Genesis 2:16-17 that God made abundant provision and then set a parameter that was for Adam and Eve's protection: "The LORD God commanded the man, saying, 'You may surely eat of every tree of the garden, but of the tree of the knowledge of good and evil you shall not eat, for in the day that you eat of it you shall surely die.'" What God provides is within his parameters and is good for us. Anything that is outside of his boundary lines can be harmful at best and, like we see above, deadly at worst.

Most of us don't like parameters (we will see that Adam and Eve were no different!). Our hearts are rebellious, and we want to be independent, autonomous, "free." But protection and provision are found within the kindness of God's good parameters.

I am aware that the concept of God as our Father can be brutally painful for some. But part of the redemptive work he does in our lives is moving into the most painful and broken places in our souls and offering us the soothing balm of his love and kindness. David wrote in Psalm 17:8, "Keep me as the apple of your eye;

hide me in the shadow of your wings." David was resting in this protective love of God and rejoicing in God's delight of him. We can do the same.

You are a cherished and greatly loved child of a perfect heavenly Father—a Father who is also the King of all kings. When God created all things good and right, his fatherly care for his children was (and is!) perfect and his relationship with them was uninterrupted. Our Father is longing for the day when we will be reunited with him in his kingdom, for the day that he can tell you and me that we are the apple of his eye—a time when we will rest perfectly in the shadow of his strong and protective wing. May the perfect love of our good Father be a deep healing balm for your soul!

THE MISSION AND DOMINION OF GOD

As we've looked at the introduction to our story (in Genesis 1–2), we have seen several important points so far:

- God is the main character—this is a story primarily about him.

- God is the King of all things—he is powerful and to be obeyed.

- God is a loving Father—he cares greatly for his children and provides abundantly for them.

In the introduction, we learn first about God. But as we learn about God, we also learn about us. We learn that he is the Creator, and we are the created; he is eternal, we are mortal; he is all-powerful, we are dependent. We learn that God gets to define what is good and set parameters where he will—and it is our job to trust and obey.

We also learn in Genesis 1–2 that God has a purpose, a mission.

And he not only called his children to participate in that mission, he also equipped them for it. God's plan was to expand his kingdom until it filled the whole earth, and he called his children to play a part in accomplishing that mission:

> God said, "Let us make man in our image, after our likeness. And let them have dominion over the fish of the sea and over the birds of the heavens and over the livestock and over all the earth and over every creeping thing that creeps on the earth." So God created man in his own image, in the image of God he created him; male and female he created them. And God blessed them. And God said to them, "Be fruitful and multiply and fill the earth and subdue it, and have dominion over the fish of the sea and over the birds of the heavens and over every living thing that moves on the earth" (Genesis 1:26-28).

God created man and woman in his image, gave them dominion, and told them to be fruitful and multiply so that they could fill the whole earth. This is a very important part of the story to know because—spoiler alert—God never changes his mind! The mission he mandated in Genesis 1–2 has never changed. Our ability to fulfill that mission has, but God is faithful, and he will finish that which he started. His purposes will not be thwarted; his mission will be completed. And just like he called Adam and Eve to participate with him, he continues to call all his people to take their place in his great mission. But, again, we're jumping ahead in the story, and we will get to that point soon enough.

The dominion God gave his children was given so they could rule over God's creation as God's representatives—rule in a way that reflected how their Father ruled over them. The creation was not for them to take and do whatever they wanted with it. Sandra Richter said it like this: "God chose to manage his creation through his representative…Thus humanity is given all authority to protect, maintain, and develop God's great gift under God's ultimate authority."[1] Adam and Eve were given work to do and that work was meaningful, satisfying, and delightful; but it was never meant to be autonomous (a do-your-own-thing mentality) in either its method or its goal. How the work was done and how the mission was to be accomplished was supposed to be both a delight to Adam and Eve as well as pleasing to their Father and King.

> We were created to do meaningful work, to accomplish, produce, contribute, and effect change—not for our own glory, but so that in everything we do, we will fill the earth with the presence of God.

God told Adam and Eve to use their dominion to go, grow, and do something, and he tells us to do the same. We were created to do meaningful work, to accomplish, produce, contribute, and effect change—not for our own glory, but so that in everything we do, we will fill the earth with the presence of God. It's vital that we understand this first glimpse of God's great mission not just so that we can "know more," but because he has called us to be participants in this same cosmic mission today—to fill the earth with his presence. How does he equip his children for this task? By creating them in his image and giving them dominion (or authority) to fulfill his mission.

IMAGE BEARING

Most of us, if not all, struggle with issues related to our identity at some point in our life. We ask questions like *Who am I? Why am I here? What is my purpose?* Well, the rock-solid foundation for our answers to those questions is found in Genesis 1—we are people created in the image of God, for his purposes and for his glory. That is made clear in Genesis 1:26-28, when God spoke to himself and said, "Let us make man in our image, after our likeness."

It is this image bearing that ultimately defines, informs, and fuels our entire purpose and goal. I like how Gregory Beale and Mitchell Kim put it:

> Adam was created in the image of the triune God to indicate his (God's) presence and rule over the earth... The Greek translation of "image" is "icon." On a computer screen, an icon is a small picture file that, when clicked, ushers in the megabytes of the computer program that it represents. Metaphorically, humanity is a small picture file in the terabytes of God's glory in creation. Although we often feel small in light of the overwhelming brokenness in the world, God has created us as icons of his powerful presence. Icons do not point to themselves, but usher in a far greater reality.[2]

In 1770, the British government had a large statue of King George III prominently placed in a park in the lower end of New York City (the soon-to-be capital of the colonies). Just days after America declared independence from Great Britain, people rushed to the statue and tore it down. Why? Why did the Brits put it there in the first place, and why did the colonists tear it down? Because both parties knew that one way to show dominion over a territory was to set up an image of the ruler over that territory. The statue of King George III represented his authority and rule over that place—to both the Brits and the Americans. So when he was no longer considered their king, the Americans quickly took his statue down!

As Christians, we are God's icons, or statues, placed all over the world. We are meant to represent him and display what it looks like to live in his kingdom. Images are supposed to (1) point to a greater reality, (2) express the dominion of the one who created the images, and, in this case, (3) create more images. Adam and Eve were called to multiply and fill the earth with more images—more people who could point to God and usher in the greater reality of his presence. You'll want to remember this point of image bearing because we will be coming back to it in chapter 9.

What does it mean to bear God's image? C. John Collins helpfully teaches that we were made with some kind of resemblance to God, which enables us to represent God both in how we rule (as those given dominion over God's creation) and in our relationships with God and others. Earlier, we briefly looked at what it means to represent God. What about resembling him?

Have you ever said something, then thought, *Oh my, I sounded just like my mother!* When my oldest daughter was three, I saw her stand at the top of the staircase, emphatically put a hand on her hip, and yell at the top of her lungs in a very authoritative manner, "Boys! Come here, right now." I knew exactly where she had heard and seen that (and it wasn't her father)! She was acting just like me.

When I am waiting in an airport, one of my favorite things to do is watch people because I love trying to figure out which children belong with which parent based on family resemblance. Image bearing was meant to mean that we so closely resembled God through how we acted, reacted, thought, lived, loved, and behaved that others would see him through us. Image bearing was meant to inform the way that we exercised our dominion—as God's representatives (more about this later). God's purpose for us as image bearers was for us to reflect his nature and character—for us to show we were "created after the likeness of God in true righteousness and holiness" (Ephesians 4:24).

Sadly, as we all know, because of humanity's fall into sin, our ability to accurately bear the image of God was deeply broken. But, as we will see, part of God's redemptive work in us is the restoration of that which was lost in the fall. Adam and Eve were created in God's image, and all who are now in Christ are being re-created to bear his image. God is restoring us to all that he intended, making us people who bear the very image of he himself.

God wants us to represent him accurately. Imagine a man starting a company and having a reputation for ethical, fair, and wise business deals. The company flourishes and is blessed with a good reputation. If the man were to pass the company on to his daughter and make her the new CEO, he would want her to continue to manage the company with the same integrity, honesty, and wisdom that he had exercised. She would be called to continue the work of the father in a way that was consistent with his vision and purpose. This is image bearing—doing the work of the Father in the same way that the Father does it.

> God is restoring us to all that he intended, making us people who bear the very image of he himself.

Points to Remember from Chapter 2

- There was a time when the world was as God intended it to be—and all of creation longs for God's order to be restored.

- The kingdom—Eden—was beautiful, peaceful, and good.

- God is the almighty, the high King of heaven and earth, the sovereign, omnipotent creator of all things— and worthy to be obeyed.

- God is the perfect Father and, as such, he provides, protects, loves, and is faithfully involved.

- God is on a mission to fill the whole earth with his presence, and he has called and equipped his children to participate in that mission with him.

- God created us in his image so that we could represent him by resembling him and be icons of his presence in all the world.

Discussion Questions

1. Read Genesis 1:3. What was the first thing God created? Describe what it might have been like to witness that event.

2. As a newly freed Israelite slave, describe how you might have possibly felt as you read the words written in Genesis 1:26-27.

3. Read Genesis 1:3, 1:6, 1:9, 1:11, 1:14, 1:20, and 1:24. What obeys God's voice? In what areas of your life does your response to "and God said" need to be "and it was so"?

4. Read Genesis 1:29. How was God being a good father to Adam and Eve?

5. Read Psalm 103:13. List some of the ways God has shown compassion to you.

6. How might you be able to use the dominion God has given you to fill a particular area of your life with the presence of God?

7. In our world today, what are some ways you see a
   longing for God's good kingdom?

8. What are some ways that people today might try to
   "tear the statues (images) down"?

9. Read Romans 8:28-30. To what are we being
   conformed? What is God using to accomplish this?
   What is the result? In what ways might that change
   how you view your current struggles?

10. Either write below or share with your group one point, truth, or lesson that either challenged or encouraged you from this chapter.

For Further Study

1. Read Psalm 104. What do you learn about God? What do you learn about creation? What do you learn about how we are to respond to both God and his creation?

2. Read Psalm 33:6-9. How is this similar to Genesis 1, and how is it different? What else do you learn about God?

3. Read Matthew 6:8. What does that phrase "your Father knows what you need before you ask him" mean? How could this truth change the way you pray?

4. Read Luke 15:11-32. Make a list of the ways God is like the father in this parable.

5. Read Colossians 1:15-20. How is Christ as the image of God different than us as an image? (hint: verse 19; John 10:30; John 14:9).

CHAPTER 3

BUT THEN AN EVIL SERPENT...

Scripture Memory

"I will put enmity between you and the woman, and between your offspring and her offspring; he shall bruise your head, and you shall bruise his heel" (Genesis 3:15).

Pray

"Deal bountifully with your servant, that I may live and keep your word. Open my eyes, that I may behold wondrous things out of your law" (Psalm 119:17-18). Father, open my eyes, not as Adam and Eve's were, but, as David prayed, open them to the glory and wonder of you and your Word.

Oh, how I long to stay in the last chapter—the part of the story when all was right in the world! But you and I know all too well that is not where we live. We no longer live in a world where the birds are always singing and the sun is always shining. Instead, we live in a world where schoolchildren and teachers are no longer safe in their classrooms, terrorists blow up buildings, and famines kill. We experience strained and broken relationships, loneliness, depression, and disappointment. We struggle to love others well; we struggle to love ourselves rightly; and we struggle to love God at all. We sit helpless in the face of disabilities, children starving, homelessness, poverty, famine, divorce, addiction, abuse, adultery, anorexia, Alzheimer's...the list could go on and on.

How do we make sense of our world—the sadness, loss, mourning, death, sickness, disease, shame, and the fact that what we long for is very different from what we experience? As these things tear our hearts apart, we wonder *Why?* and *How long?* We weep and mourn and grieve. Or we shake our fists in anger and walk away from God. Most of us don't have a category in which to put suffering and sadness and have a hard time making sense of them. We intuitively know things are not the way they are supposed to be—and there is a deep longing in us to return to that time when all was right in the world. What has happened?

Understanding both what we've already seen about the way it was supposed to be, as well as what we are about to study—the great disruption in the "way it was supposed to be"—is the only way to make sense of our lives today and to be people that, yes, grieve, but not as those who grieve without hope.

Every year, my friend's two daughters are in a Christmas play at their church. To call it a play might conjure up images of *The Best Christmas Pageant Ever*—a classic story of makeshift sets and homemade costumes. But this is no low-rent show! It is more like going to see a Broadway production. The costumes and makeup are spectacular, the singing and dancing are professional, and live animals are all across the stage.

The opening scene depicts the creation of the world. The actors, in makeup and costumes like those in the Broadway production of *The Lion King*, become animals that leap, bound, hop, run, crawl, somersault, and fly from all parts of the church up to the stage. Our hearts soar with the music. It is a beautiful scene of the creation rejoicing in its Creator.

But all of a sudden, the lights dim and the church grows dark.

The music changes from jubilant to sinister. From the back of the building, a large snake-like creature begins to wind its way through the crowd, slithering slowly toward the stage where Adam, Eve, and all of creation cower in fear. There is no doubt that something is about to happen—something that is not right, not good, and not the way it is supposed to be.

THE INTRUDER

There is a point in almost every story when you realize something has happened that will permanently alter the course of the plot. As we read our story, we can almost hear the change in the music. It's as if the birds stop singing and the sky darkens as we read the jarring words, "Now the serpent was more crafty than any other beast of the field that the LORD God had made" (Genesis 3:1).

When I am watching my friend's daughters reenact this scene, there is no doubt for those in the audience that the serpent is intruding on the scene as an unwelcome, uninvited, and unintended visitor. And that is how we are supposed to read the opening words of Genesis 3. There is a clear disconnect between the first two chapters of Genesis and the third. As Michael Williams says:

> Scripture proclaims categorically that sin is an intruder. It is not the product of God's creativity. It does not belong...Nor does Genesis seek to make sense of sin... Sin remains ever a riddle, ever absurd, ever irrational. Augustine quite rightly said that seeking a rational explanation for the origin of sin is like trying to see darkness or hear silence.[1]

And that is what we see in Genesis 3. We are left wondering why, but there is no rational answer because sin is irrational. Adam and Eve had everything they were created to want. Their rebellion made no sense. They rebelled against a good, loving, providing, faithful, relational, Father-King who had given them everything they could want or need.

The first seven verses of Genesis 3 depict a strange scene:

> Now the serpent was more crafty than any other beast of the field that the LORD God had made. He said to the woman, "Did God actually say, 'You shall not eat of any tree in the garden'?" And the woman said to the serpent, "We may eat of the fruit of the trees in the garden, but God said, 'You shall not eat of the fruit of the tree that is in the midst of the garden, neither shall you touch it, lest you die.'" But the serpent said to the woman, "You will not surely die. For God knows that when you eat of it your eyes will be opened, and you will be like God, knowing good and evil." So when the woman saw that the tree was good for food, and that it was a delight to the eyes, and that the tree was to be desired to make one wise, she took of its fruit and ate, and she also gave some to her husband who was with her, and he ate. Then the eyes of both were opened, and they knew that they were naked. And they sewed fig leaves together and made themselves loincloths.

As faithful readers, we are supposed to feel the absurdity of it all. We are supposed to be puzzled and scratch our heads because sin should always confound us. Unfortunately, in the same way we can read this verse with a familiarity that numbs us to its absurdity, we can also grow very accustomed to sin itself, so accustomed that it starts to feel normal. It's not. As Williams said, sin is an intruder. But to call it an intruder means that sin is not just some nebulous force or random "thing" floating around in the air that we should try to avoid. Sin is anchored in something, someone, this "intruder." But who is this crafty serpent in Genesis 3?

The book of Revelation mentions some of the events that will occur at the end of the story of redemption. There, we read that a day is coming when this will have happened: "the great dragon was thrown down, that ancient serpent, who is called the devil and Satan, the deceiver of the whole world—he was thrown down to the earth, and his angels were thrown down with him" (Revelation 12:9). Many people think of God and Satan as equally matched foes—enemies across the table from each other in some kind of eternal chess match. But that is not how Scripture portrays them. Enemies, yes. But equals, absolutely not!

But we're not there yet. We live in between the events of Genesis 3 and Revelation 12. So how do we live now? How do we stand against the one who defeated Adam and Eve? Well, God does not leave us alone. He gives us real weapons and real help:

> Finally, be strong in the Lord and in the strength of his might. Put on the whole armor of God, that you may be able to stand against the schemes of the devil. For we do not wrestle against flesh and blood, but against the rulers, against the authorities, against the cosmic powers over this present darkness, against the spiritual forces of evil in the heavenly places. Therefore take up the whole armor of God, that you may be able to withstand in the evil day, and having done all, to stand firm. Stand therefore, having fastened on the belt of truth, and having put on the breastplate of righteousness, and, as shoes for your feet, having put on the readiness given by the gospel of peace. In all circumstances take up the shield of faith, with which you can extinguish all the flaming darts of the evil one; and take the

helmet of salvation, and the sword of the Spirit, which
is the word of God (Ephesians 6:10-17).

At the very end of the story (which is the beginning of forever—
we'll get there later in this book!), we read that "the devil who had
deceived them was thrown into the lake of fire and sulfur where
the beast and the false prophet were, and they will be tormented
day and night forever and ever" (Revelation 20:10). The day is
coming, friend, when the intruder, the enemy of our souls, will be
forever banished and all the evil he has inflicted will be gone. That
day will be here before we know it, so hang on. Our God wins.

THE SIN

Here it is—the point in the story that changes everything. It
is akin to Snow White's teeth sinking into the apple or Sleeping
Beauty's finger reaching out and touching the needle, or Scar killing Mufasa—there is no going back. Have you ever watched a movie and, knowing what is going to happen, wanted to yell at the characters on the screen, "No! don't do it!" That is how we should feel upon reading the first several verses of Genesis 3. We should want to tell Eve to stop talking with that snake, stop listening to his ideas, and, for goodness' sake, put that fruit down.

> The day is coming, friend, when the intruder, the enemy of our souls, will be forever banished and all the evil he has inflicted will be gone.

But, instead, I think most of us wonder what the big deal is
about eating some fruit. Why did so much devastation come from
something that we might do every day? And if God had made the
fruit, why was it so wrong to eat it? Was the fruit the issue?

The fruit in and of itself was not the problem. In Genesis 2, we read that God had generously given Adam and Eve many trees with much fruit, an abundance of riches, and, in addition to everything else, he had given them access to the tree of life.

- "Out of the ground the LORD God made to spring up every tree that is pleasant to the sight and good for food. The tree of life was in the midst of the garden, and the tree of the knowledge of good and evil" (Genesis 2:9).

- "The name of the first is the Pishon. It is the one that flowed around the whole land of Havilah, where there is gold. And the gold of that land is good; bdellium and onyx stone are there" (Genesis 2:11-12).

- "The LORD God commanded the man, saying, 'You may surely eat of every tree of the garden'" (Genesis 2:16).

But, out of all the good things that God freely gave Adam and Eve, he sovereignly chose to prohibit one thing—the tree of the knowledge of good and evil: "Of the tree of the knowledge of good and evil you shall not eat, for in the day that you eat of it you shall surely die" (Genesis 2:17). Many, many trees were in the garden for their delight, and only one was forbidden.

And, oh, the same temptation is there for all of us! We underemphasize what God has given and overemphasize what God has prohibited. Gratitude and contentment are difficult, while complaining and discontentment seem to come so easily. Culturally, we are surrounded by a lack of contentment, even encouraged to be discontent. Think of all the ways that commercials are targeted at this proclivity in us to be discontent with what we do have and stir up in us a longing for that which we don't have.

I have been convicted recently to actively combat this tendency in myself. Psalm 16:6 has become my mantra: "The lines have fallen for me in pleasant places; indeed, I have a beautiful inheritance." I say this when I am tempted to want that which the Lord has chosen not to give or to wish that he hadn't given what he has. I am actively trying to choose gratitude and thanksgiving to replace my feelings of ingratitude and complaining. But the true sin, the true temptation that the enemy enticed Eve with was not discontentment—although, like he does with us, he used it to lead her to the place of rebellion.

In Genesis 2:17, God told Adam that if he were to eat the fruit of the forbidden tree, he would "surely die." In Genesis 3:4-5, Satan told Eve that if she were to eat the fruit of the forbidden tree, she would "not surely die." And this lie continues to be whispered to us today—the lie that says God cannot be trusted and his Word is simply not true. One thing we can say about Satan: He is neither original nor creative. He keeps whispering the same lie over and over to us in new situations—but the lie itself is not new.

One question most of us ask is, Why did God give Adam and Eve the prohibition in the first place? Why didn't they have total freedom to do whatever they wanted? We must remember that Adam and Eve were not created to live autonomously, independently, or self-centeredly; they were created to live in right relationship with their Creator. Adam and Eve were given both privilege and responsibility. They were created to resemble and reflect their Father, the King. And both kings and fathers are to be obeyed. God had every right to set a boundary on them and his created order— this was his world. Sandra Richter says, "In essence, Adam and Eve are free to do anything except decide for themselves what is good and what is evil. Yahweh reserves the right (and the responsibility) to name those truths for himself."[2] Obedience is always part of the arrangement between fathers and children and between kings and their subjects. God is being God—a good father and a good king—and his boundaries are wise and good.

Genesis 2 closed with the beautiful words, "The man and his wife were both naked and were not ashamed" (verse 25). Then in Genesis 3, the serpent promised them that "when you eat of [the fruit] your eyes will be opened, and you will be like God, knowing good and evil" (verse 5). After Adam and Eve disobeyed, we read that their eyes were opened all right, but the result was far from what had been promised: "The eyes of both were opened, and they knew that they were naked" (verse 7).

Have you ever experienced something like this? Has the enemy ever whispered a promise in your ear on the front end of a sin, and then, on the other side, the place from which you cannot undo what has been done, you realized that promise was a lie? Of course it was a lie! That is the language of our enemy. Jesus said that "he [the devil] was a murderer from the beginning, and does not stand in the truth, because there is no truth in him. When he lies, he speaks out of his own character, for he is a liar and the father of lies" (John 8:44).

But, oh, how we long to believe him sometimes. What he promises seems to be just what we desire or think we need. If he is currently trying to convince you that God's Word is not true or that your life would be richer if you disobeyed, then run! Run the other way. If you do not run when Satan lies, you will get to the other side and feel the same shame and fear that Adam and Eve felt.

This is the saddest part of the story. And, really, it should be the end of the story. As one of my professors said, the story should be God made it, man broke it, the end. But the glorious hope of the gospel is that humanity's fall into sin was not the end. Keep reading, and see the grace of our mighty God!

THE SHAME

When my son was about three years old, he found some cookies he knew he was not supposed to eat. I found him hiding in the front hall closet, happily munching away. When I opened the door, he quickly hid the box of cookies behind his back and looked up at me with big eyes and a concerned expression (fear) on his face—and crumbs on his lips.

He had hidden to commit the crime, and then tried to hide the evidence of the crime itself. Isn't that the nature of sin? Usually while we are committing it, we know it's wrong, so our tendency is to hide as we're sinning. Then afterward, we try to cover up the evidence of the sin we have committed.

To get the cookies out of the pantry, my son had to make sure no one was in the room—he had to sneak. In the same way, we have to whisper a lie, or say it behind closed doors, so we hide what we are saying from others. If a person is going to shoplift, he or she has to make sure no one is looking. If someone is going to commit adultery, he or she has to figure out a way to hide their activity from others. Most sins are not committed in broad daylight. Hiding is a part of sin. If you feel the urge to hide something, you need to stop and ask yourself why.

Part of what we see in Genesis 3 is that hiding from God is not possible. God later asked Jeremiah, "Can a man hide himself in secret places so that I cannot see him? declares the LORD. Do I not fill heaven and earth? declares the LORD" (Jeremiah 23:24). And it is good, good news that we can't hide from the Lord!

There is a little word in Scripture that can make all the difference in the world. It is the word *but*, and it is used when the author wants to introduce a point that is in complete contrast to what has just been said. We see that usage in Genesis 3:9. Adam and Eve were hiding, "*but* the LORD God called to the man and said to him, 'Where are you?'" (emphasis added).

Have you ever asked yourself what would have happened if God hadn't done that? If the story just ended in Genesis 3:8 with "the man and his wife hid themselves from the presence of the LORD God among the trees of the garden"? Adam and Eve would have been lost forever. But the good news is that God did call out to them, and he went to "find" them! He pursued his children even though they were running from him. God entered the place of their disobedience.

As we've already seen, now that sin has entered the picture, so has shame. There are different kinds of shame—shame we experience for things we've done, things done to us, and even things about us. And shame is a terrible weapon in the hands of our enemy. Shame can keep us from being in relationship with others, and even in relationship with God—no wonder the enemy wields it so powerfully in our lives. Shame makes us want to hide; shame tells us that we should hide. But, praise be to our good and loving Father-God, he does not leave us in the misery of our shame.

Like the day I found my son in the closet, there were many times that I had to kneel in front of my children, put my hand gently under their chin, and lift their head to look at me. They were ashamed of what they had done, and didn't want to make eye contact. I have felt that same way many times with God. But praise be to our God, for he is a God who time and again will stoop down, take our face in his hands, lift our face back up to his, and remove our shame. Psalm 3:3 says, "You, O LORD, are a shield about me, my glory, and the lifter of my head."

Just like sin usually leads to shame, shame usually leads to blame. You may have heard someone say, "The devil made me do it." People usually say this in a joking manner, but the message conveyed is that I'm not responsible for my own wrongdoings, and sin isn't my fault because "the devil made me do it." What a sweet relief it is to blame someone else!

> One of the most glorious parts of our story is that Jesus came not only to forgive our sin and take our blame, but to call us out of hiding and remove our shame!

Our desire to blame someone or something else presents itself in many ways. From "The dog ate my homework" to telling your coworkers that your mistake was a technical glitch, a missed memo, or the fault of a boss who didn't clearly communicate the expectations, we're all familiar with the blame game. The threat of experiencing the shame that comes with our sins, faults, errors, and mistakes is a powerful force. No one wants to feel shame. But blame is actually not the way to alleviate shame.

At the end of Genesis 2, we saw a beautiful picture of how Adam and Eve were "both naked and were not ashamed." There is so much freedom conveyed in that short verse. This freedom and self-forgetfulness were lost once sin entered the story. But one of the most glorious parts of our story is that Jesus came not only to forgive our sin and take our blame, but to call us out of hiding and remove our shame! He came to us in the exact place of our disobedience, willing to restore all that shame tries to steal from us. If he is calling you and asking you to come out of hiding, run to him. He is safe, he is loving, and he is ready to forgive you.

THE SENTENCE

If you were the defendant in a criminal case, I imagine the worst part of the trial would be waiting for the sentence to be given. Especially if, despite making the best case possible to avoid punishment, you knew you were guilty.

That is what happened in Genesis 3:14-19. God sentenced those who had done wrong. Think about what it would have been like to wait for the Judge to speak the words that would define the rest of your life. And the scope of this sentence isn't just the rest of Adam's life, or Eve's life, or my life, or your life—it is for all of creation until kingdom come.

Why is that so? Why do we all suffer the consequences of Adam and Eve's sin? I'm sure you have heard people say things like, "Thanks a lot, Eve!" Or express confidence that they would have done differently and not take that forbidden bite. Many people wonder why the rest of us have to suffer because Adam and Eve sinned.

Theologically, this is one of the most important concepts we can understand: the idea that one person stands as the representative of a larger group, and what goes for the representative goes for the group.

We all know, at some level, what this is like. My daughters played basketball, and before a game started, the team captain would go out to meet the other team captain and shake hands. These captains were representing their respective teams. The gesture of goodwill and sportsmanship given with the shaking of hands meant not just that the two captains were pledging to play fairly, but their teams were too. Their actions were on behalf of the whole team because they were the representatives.

Likewise, when the president of the United States signs a peace treaty, he is signing it on behalf of all US citizens because he is the representative head of our country—his actions will result in peace, or war, for all those who are represented by him. On the negative side of representation, consider the CEO of a company who makes a bad financial decision, and the company fails as a result. All those under that CEO's leadership will lose their jobs. The actions of one will have an impact on all those that person represents.

We see this over and over again in the Old Testament with the kings of Israel: As the kings go, so goes the nation. Good kings bring peace and prosperity, and evil kings bring disaster and hardship. While we may think that it is unfair, we live with this reality all the time. In addition, and more importantly, our salvation is wrapped up in the fact that we have a representative. But, again, that is jumping ahead in our story!

Adam was the representative head of all humanity. As a result, the sentence given to Adam and Eve is our sentence too. But before God pronounced judgment on his children, he first promised that there would be redemption from the consequences he was about to give.

God began handing out consequences by speaking to the serpent first. And he began with both a curse and a promise. In Genesis 3:15, God drew the battle line and vowed to send someone who would utterly defeat the serpent. Amazingly, even after Adam and Eve's rebellion and sin, God was promising to do battle not against his children, but for them. This is our first glimpse of the gospel. And it is the good news that punishment will not be God's ultimate answer to sin, but redemption. God promised to defeat the one who had just defeated them.

After God dealt with the serpent, he turned to the woman, and then the man. He gave them the punishment for their disobedience. From this moment on, all people would experience life under this curse. There would be pain in childbearing, conflict in marriage, frustration in work, and, ultimately, physical death. And don't we feel the weight of these things every single day?

In Genesis 1:28, God called Adam and Eve to be fruitful, multiply, and fill the earth. Now they would struggle to do all three. C. John Collins points out that the "joyful task of 'multiplying' (1:28) becomes the arena of 'multiplied' pain (3:16) and the sphere in which humans were supposed to experience God's blessing (multiplying) is now 'an arena of [multiplied] pain, danger, and curse.'"[3] And don't we know, all too well, the truth of his words. The pain associated with multiplying is extensive. We tend to think only the physical pain associated with birthing a child is in view here, but this pain encompasses everything from infertility to miscarriage, from the loss of a child to unmet longings for a child, and from complications in pregnancy to childhood illness. It has in view all the pain, heartache, and anxiety that goes along with "multiplying" in this broken world.

If you are married, know anyone who is married, or long to be married, Genesis 3:16 should explain much. The wonderful institution of marriage—invented, ordained, and blessed by God—is a realm in which we intimately experience the results of the fall. Whether it is strife in our parents' marriage or our own, the yet unmet desire to be married, the devastation of divorce, or the myriad ways we encounter sexual brokenness, most of us have experienced difficulties relating to marriage. In Genesis 2 we saw joy, delight, deep satisfaction, and safe vulnerability between the man and woman. We saw perfect harmony between two people. They were different but were created to be co-heirs of the kingdom and co-workers in advancing the kingdom. And, until Genesis 3, everything indicates that there was no strife. Eve didn't rebel and usurp, and Adam didn't dominate and dictate. They worked shoulder to shoulder with joy and love. But in Genesis 3 we are told they will oppose each other. Things will not be the way they are supposed to be.

No matter how many times I say things are not the way they are supposed to be, do I mean that there is nothing we can do in response, or that we are to have a resigned attitude and wait things out? No! We are called to push back the curse, reverse it, and press into the beauty of a redeemed world and redeemed relationships. As we pray, "Your kingdom come [now]…on earth as it is in heaven" (Matthew 6:10), we are meant to participate with that prayer! We are to fight against fighting. Married or not, we are to learn what it means to fight for the marriages around us, not against them. For some, this means learning to speak positively about your own or your friend's spouse. For others (to put it bluntly), it means to stop flirting with someone else's spouse. It means praying for the marriages in our churches and neighborhoods. It means living in sexual integrity—whether we are married or single—in all areas. If you are married, it means you strive to work alongside your spouse, not against them. It means marriage counseling with an eye toward humility and restoration. It means that we participate with our Father in the business of restoring all things, including the brokenness in marriages—ours and those around us.

THE MERCY

When my children were young, there were a handful of times that their disobedience required tough discipline, and my concern for their ultimate good compelled me to love them enough to administer that discipline. I can vividly remember a time when one child was requiring some "tough love" and the discipline Craig and I were giving felt severe. We removed many privileges and instituted many restrictions. The situation was hard. But it was not anger that motivated us to do what we did; great love for our child was our motivation. And through the whole ordeal (and it was an *ordeal*), Craig and I did not pull back from this child relationally; instead, we were able to hold him, remind him of our love and care for him, and tell him that we were actually "for him" in all of this. The consequences were given—and implemented—but the relationship was not severed. And in a much bigger, better way, that is what we see in Genesis 3.

After God pronounced judgment, we read this: "The man called his wife's name Eve, because she was the mother of all living. And the LORD God made for Adam and for his wife garments of skins and clothed them" (Genesis 3:20-21). God was still caring for his children, and he was reminding Eve, through Adam, that the call on her life was still in effect! She had not lost her status as co-heir of the kingdom, and the calling to have dominion over the creation in a way that brings life and flourishing was still a part of what God had created her to do. For her to fulfill her calling would be a lot more difficult now; she would struggle with wanting to have dominion not with her husband, but over her husband. She would struggle with pain in multiplying, but God said she would still have the privilege of being not just a life-giver, but the mother of all who will live. God is the God of all mercy—then and now!

Adam and Eve had received a punishment that was both just and merciful, and they had received a word of hope—this curse and punishment would not be the end; God was going to act on their behalf to crush the one who had just defeated them. But, even though they had attempted to cover themselves, they were still standing there wearing those ridiculous little fig leaves, feeling the weight of their shame. Can you relate? I can.

I am a woman who lives "post sin" far more often than I wish, and for me, Genesis 3:21 conveys one of the sweetest moments in all of Scripture. Remember how Adam and Eve felt before their sin? They were naked and not ashamed. But after their sin, they hid because they realized they were naked, and they felt ashamed. Shame is what makes us want to hide; it makes us feel exposed.

Now, there is a shame that is good and right, the kind we feel before we confess sin and repent of it. That shame will drive us to God. But shame not associated with our sin, or shame that persists after we have confessed and repented, is a tool our enemy uses to drive us away from God.

Do you ever feel like your past sins have disqualified you from kingdom service? Praise be to God, they don't! Repented sin is forgiven sin; forgiven sin is covered sin. The apostle Paul, the man who identified himself as the chief of sinners, also wrote almost half of the New Testament. So he knew what he was talking about when he wrote, "There is therefore now no condemnation for those who are in Christ Jesus" (Romans 8:1).

> Like Adam and Eve, we are completely dependent on God moving toward us, covering us, providing for us. And that is exactly what he did and still does.

God moved toward Adam and Eve in tenderness to cover what was now the source of their shame their nakedness. This was a moment between a perfect Father and his wayward children. This was tenderness and love in the midst of discipline. It was a moment that displayed God's care and provision for both real and felt needs. Like Adam and Eve, we are completely dependent on God moving toward us, covering us, providing for us. And that is exactly what he did and still does.

So why couldn't the problem end right there? Adam and Eve had received consequences, so why couldn't they go back to the way things were? Why did they have to be kicked out of the garden?

> The LORD God said, "Behold, the man has become like one of us in knowing good and evil. Now, lest he reach out his hand and take also of the tree of life and eat, and live forever—" therefore the LORD God sent him out from the garden of Eden to work the ground from which he was taken (Genesis 3:22-23).

My favorite explanation is from C.F. Keil: "The expulsion from paradise, therefore, was a punishment inflicted *for man's good*, intended, while exposing him to temporal death, to preserve him from eternal death"[4] (emphasis added).

It is so important that we understand this! God, in his mercy, did not want to leave his children in their state of sin and suffering. Because of his mercy, he sent them out of the garden to prevent them from eating from the tree of life. If they had not been expelled and still had access to the tree, they would have forever and ever and ever and ever had to deal with their sin and shame. They would have lived forever as sinful, fallen people.

We all long for the day we will be delivered from our sin—not just the penalty of our sin, but its power and presence in us. And it will be our physical death that ushers us into that state. So banning Adam and Eve from the tree of life was mercy indeed. Because God did this, we have the glorious hope of one day being delivered from this body of death, reunited with God, and then—only then—will we again have access to the tree of life. How merciful is our God!

Points to Remember from Chapter 3

- God reserves the right to define what is good and what is evil.

- Our enemy always tempts us to doubt God's word and his goodness.

- Sin is irrational, illogical, absurd, and alien—it is not part of the way life is supposed to be.

- Sin leads to shame and hiding, but God calls us out and covers us.

- Punishment is not God's ultimate answer to sin; redemption is.

- God, in his mercy, will not leave us in the state of sin forever.

Discussion Questions

1. Read Genesis 3:1. List what you learn about the serpent. What were the first four words the serpent uttered? Ponder those words for a moment, and describe how they make you feel.

2. Read Ephesians 6:10-18. List all the action verbs that indicate what we are commanded to do. How might these help you fight against the temptations to doubt or disobey?

3. Read Jeremiah 23:23-24. Praise God that we cannot hide from him! In light of what you read in this chapter, what do the lyrics "I once was lost, but now am found" mean to you?

4. Read Genesis 3:14-19. Who is the only one speaking? What does this indicate about authority (imagine if this were a court of law)?

5. Punishment is not God's ultimate answer to sin—
   redemption is. What does this mean to you? What is
   the right response to this truth?

6. What are some ways you can work to "push back" the
   curse?

7. Read Genesis 3:21. In what ways do you see the Lord
   caring for his children while still disciplining them?

8. Read Genesis 3:20. If you are reading a study Bible, the notes for this verse will likely tell you that Eve's name means "life giver." Why is that a particularly hopeful fact to know in light of the curse?

9. Either write below or share with your group one point, truth, or lesson that either challenged or encouraged you from this chapter.

For Further Study

1. Read Genesis 3:1 and compare the serpent's words with what God said in Genesis 2:16-17. What did the serpent do to God's words?

2. Read 2 Corinthians 11:3. What was Paul (the author of 2 Corinthians) concerned would happen? Where does the battle take place? How has this been true in your life?

3. Read John 8:44. What three points did Jesus make about the devil? How do we see the truth of these points in Genesis 3:1-5?

4. Read Psalm 139:1-12. Do you agree with David that "such knowledge [about how well God knows you] is too wonderful" (verse 6), or does it unnerve you to think that you cannot hide from God? Why?

5. Read John 19:2. What did Jesus wear on his head? Thinking about Genesis 3:17-18, why might it be significant that what he wore on his head was made of thorns?

6. There are several famous works of art that depict the expulsion from the garden. Unfortunately, most show Adam and Eve cowering in fear and shame—which misses the fact this was an act of God's mercy and grace. One person wrote, as an explanation for Doré's piece, "As punishment for abusing his trust, God drives Adam and Eve from the Garden of Eden... Adam and Eve are on their own from now on." But, based on what we studied in this chapter, why is this not an accurate depiction of what we read in Scripture?

CHAPTER 4

THE HEART OF OUR KING

Scripture Memory

"I will walk among you and will be your God, and you shall be my people" (Leviticus 26:12).

Pray

> *"Know therefore that the LORD your God is God, the*
> *faithful God who keeps covenant and steadfast love*
> *with those who love him and keep his commandments,*
> *to a thousand generations" (Deuteronomy 7:9).*
> *Father, thank you for your steadfast, unfailing*
> *love and your covenantal faithfulness to me.*

Genesis 3 ended the way it began—abruptly and disruptively. It was definitely not the high point of the story! The people we identify with most in the story were defeated and cast out of the garden. And they were incapable of remedying their situation. They couldn't fight their way back in, they couldn't earn their way back in, and the death they were told would come would conquer them if they didn't get back in. But they were created for the goodness of Eden—perfect fellowship with God, each other, themselves, and creation. The only way their situation could be remedied and they could be restored to the goodness of the garden was for someone to rescue them.

You might be wondering if we are now going to move on to Genesis chapter 4, and, if so, how we are going to get through the whole story within the pages of this book. I promise you that we are not going to go chapter by chapter through the Bible (even though that would be fascinating)! But the reason we spent so much time studying the first three chapters of the Bible is because the events that took place in them are so crucial to our understanding of the entire story. We can't see the tragedy of the dilemma if we don't see God's original intent, and we can't see the glory of the solution if we don't know the dilemma.

So far, we have seen that God created the world and all that is in it (including mankind), and he called it very good. Yet our experience tells us that all is no longer very good. And now we know why: Sin entered this good creation and disrupted it to the core. But the good news is that the brokenness, pain, suffering, and evil that we currently live with have both a beginning point in the story and, as we will soon see, an end!

We have already seen God's promise to fix this deep disruption. His solution will involve the seed (or offspring) of the woman and will result in the destruction of the enemy. The story has been set for intrigue and adventure. We know the setting, we know the conflict, and we have been given a glimpse of the great resolution. As we pick up the pace and trace the key moments in the story, we will first turn our attention to the heart of our Father, the way of our Father, and the promises of our Father in order to understand why he does what he does, how he does it, and what we learn about him in the midst of the greatest rescue of all time.

THE HEART OF THE KING—LOVE

Does it help you to know what compels a person to act? Earlier this week as I was writing this book, my husband brought home a beautiful bouquet of flowers. And, as lovely as his gift was, don't you think knowing why he brought them to me would make a difference in how I responded to the gift? Was he feeling guilty? Did he feel obliged to get the flowers? Did he think his gift would produce some great effect on our marriage? Were the flowers even for me? Yes, they were for me, and yes, he brought them because he loves me (and also because the bouquet he had brought to me the previous week had wilted). Understanding his heart helped me to better appreciate his action.

In the same way, knowing what compels God to act helps us to understand and appreciate his action. Why did he embark on this great rescue mission? Why didn't he just leave us to our own plight? Was he obliged to rescue us? Was it pity that compelled him? Did he stand to gain anything by rescuing us? Here, I quote Paul: "By no means!" (see, for example, Romans 6:2). God was in no way obliged, nor did he stand to gain anything. Quite the opposite was true—this cost him greatly! And even though God's mercy toward us is great, it wasn't pity that compelled him to rescue us.

In Deuteronomy 7:6-8, God, spoke through Moses to the people he had just redeemed out of Egypt, and told them,

> You are a people holy to the LORD your God. The LORD your God has chosen you to be a people for his treasured possession, out of all the peoples who are on the face of the earth. It was not because you were more in number than any other people that the LORD set his love on you and chose you, for you were the fewest of

> all peoples, but it is because the LORD loves you and
> is keeping the oath that he swore to your fathers, that
> the LORD has brought you out with a mighty hand and
> redeemed you from the house of slavery, from the hand
> of Pharaoh king of Egypt.

The exodus (or exit) out of Egypt—when God delivered his people out of bondage and slavery—is the great rescue mission in the Old Testament. God references it repeatedly throughout the story, and this is meant to typify, or to give a foretaste of, the even greater rescue mission that he would perform through Jesus Christ. So, when God told the Israelites they hadn't done anything to compel him to rescue them, we can appropriate the same thought to his even greater rescue of us. God did not rescue us because we are great, wonderful, strong, or even cute. He rescued us because of his great love.

If you know anyone who has gone through the adoption process, you understand a bit of this kind of love. When a family sets out to adopt a child, they embark on a difficult journey. There are papers to be filled out, checks to be written, hands that are wrung, prayers that are prayed, and time that is consumed. But during this process, what is the child doing? Nothing! What can the child do? He can't fill out the paperwork, write any checks, or even look through a list of potential parents and select one. Rather, the child is dependent on the love and actions of their future parents. How similar, and yet how much greater, is the story of our adoption.

> God did not rescue us because we are great, wonderful, strong, or even cute. He rescued us because of his great love.

God, compelled by his great love for us, did everything necessary to make us his own.

THE WAY OF THE KING—COVENANT

Does it matter to you whether my husband and I are married, or we are simply living together outside of marriage? It should (for so many reasons)! But why? Why isn't it enough for us to know that we love each other? What is the difference between marriage and living together? The difference is a covenant. The covenant that I entered with Craig Doctor on a cold January day in 1990 provides the framework for understanding the nature of our commitment. Yes, we love each other, but it is the covenant of marriage that binds us together.

When we entered that covenant, we had to make promises to each other about how we would act in the future—and those promises bind us to one another and to the one to whom we made the promises. We promised that no matter what happened—sickness or health, riches or poverty, joy or sorrow—we would love and cherish each other until one of us died. And to symbolize our commitment; we gave each other rings. Love compelled us to enter this covenant, but it is the covenant that defines the nature of our relationship: We are bound to each other.

In a much greater (perfect even) way, God binds himself to us with covenants. Love compelled him; covenant binds him. Michael Williams said it like this: "God's way in all this [the story of redemption]…is the way of covenant."[1] Covenant is the way that God goes about accomplishing his purposes—he makes certain promises to his people, and then he binds himself to those promises. Our God is a covenant-making and covenant-keeping God.

While we are somewhat familiar with the idea of what a covenant is (think of words like *promise, contract, pledge,* and *commitment*), we also live in an age of no-fault divorce, cohabitation instead of marriage, and shameless adultery. This can jade and slant our thoughts on what a covenant really is, and the strength of the bond that is intended.

Covenants were part of the ancient world, the world of the Old Testament. The most common type of covenant was called a suzerain-vassal covenant, in which the suzerain, or stronger party (think nation or king), pledged to protect and provide for the weaker party, or vassal. In return for that protection, the vassal promised obedience and loyalty. In this arrangement, a larger and mightier kingdom promised to protect a smaller and weaker kingdom and, in exchange, the smaller kingdom would be loyal and offer support.

These covenants were typically ratified, or entered into, with a ceremony. During the ceremony, animals were slaughtered, cut in half, and laid on opposite sides of a path. Both parties would then walk the bloody path between the animals that had been cut in two. As they did, they would pledge loyalty to their side of the covenant—provision and protection, or obedience and faithfulness.

God used a concept familiar to the ancient Israelites to help them understand what he was doing. He would be their suzerain, and they were to be his vassal. He was the initiator of the covenant because he was the stronger party. He would provide and protect and, because his people were the weaker party, they were to pledge loyalty and obedience.

But why? Why would an omniscient, sovereign, faithful God bind himself to an unfaithful people?

The factor that compelled God to do this is captured in multiple places throughout the story, including

Leviticus 26:12: "I will walk among you and will be your God, and you shall be my people."

Jeremiah 30:22: "You shall be my people, and I will be your God."

Ezekiel 36:28: "You shall dwell in the land that I gave to your fathers, and you shall be my people, and I will be your God."

This is possibly one of the greatest truths we can understand about our God and our story. This great rescue mission is for a purpose: God wants to be our God and wants us to be his people. In other words, he wants to be in relationship with us! He loves us. And so he binds himself to his own promises, knowing that is the only one who will be faithful and keep the covenant. Our faithful God entered into a binding relationship with unfaithful people. He knew on the front end that he would have to be the one upholding both sides of the covenant, and because he is faithful, he keeps his promises and accomplishes his will. We are his people, and he is our God.

Covenant is our God's binding promise to be our God and to make us his own—to redeem a people for himself. That is God's mission. But even though God has only one mission, did he make only one covenant for the accomplishment of that mission? No. He made multiple covenants. God entered covenants with Adam, Noah, Abram, Moses, David, and, of course, us—we have the new covenant through Jesus.

How are we to think about the fact that God entered multiple covenants? Does God change his mind or alter his course? No! God's promise remains the same: to redeem a people for himself. But each covenant gives a little more information about how he will do that, what his people should be looking for, and how they are to respond. Each covenant builds on the ones before and gives a little more information about God's great rescue mission. In this chapter, we will trace the covenants through the Old Testament.

TRACING THE COVENANTS—NOAH

Look at Genesis 3:15 again: "I will put enmity between you and the woman, and between your offspring and her offspring; he shall bruise your head, and you shall bruise his heel." Both the ESV and the NIV use the word "offspring." The Hebrew word is *zera'*, and it can also be translated "seed" or "descendant." The verse goes on to say that "*he* [this offspring] shall bruise your head and you shall bruise *his* heel" (emphasis added).

The first promise given is that there will be a descendant of Adam—a man, a singular human being—who will crush the head of the enemy. This is of utmost importance. As we trace the covenants, we will be tracing the seed of the woman. The Bible goes to great lengths to show that God's promise continues through the offspring of Adam and Eve. Look for words like *seed, offspring, son, children,* and *generations.*

After Adam and Eve were expelled from the garden, we see sin abound in the next eight chapters of Genesis. The beauty of the garden was lost. Cain murdered Abel, Lamech killed numerous men, and corruption overflowed. The question we should be asking as we read about this persistent downward spiral is, Did sin win? God had promised in Genesis 3:15 that he would win, but all we read about after the garden is sin abounding. Then God sent the flood. Did his promise survive the destruction? Would our covenant-keeping God still be faithful to his word? Would the seed of the woman survive?

When we read Genesis 6–9, the account of Noah and the flood, we need to hear God shouting from the mountaintops that he will forever be faithful to his word, and he will accomplish all he has promised to do. Nothing will triumph over him, especially not sin and corruption. As Michael Williams says:

> Sin and judgment is at best only half the story...The point is rather to communicate God's resolve to redeem in spite of fallen man, and that sin cannot thwart the promise made in the Garden. It is about grace, that God will protect the seed of the woman and will affect his plan to redeem in spite of sin's power and allure. Like all of Scripture, the story is about the faithfulness of God.[2]

The flood destroyed almost everything. But God, again, like he did in the garden, saved in the midst of his judgment. One man and his family survived. And with that one man, Noah, God reestablished his creation purpose and entered into covenant with humankind.

> God said, "This is the sign of the covenant that I make between me and you and every living creature that is with you, for all future generations: I have set my bow in the cloud, and it shall be a sign of the covenant between me and the earth. When I bring clouds over the earth and the bow is seen in the clouds, I will remember my covenant that is between me and you and every living creature of all flesh. And the waters shall never again become a flood to destroy all flesh. When the bow is in the clouds, I will see it and remember the everlasting covenant between God and every living creature of all flesh that is on the earth." God said to Noah, "This is the sign of the covenant that I have established between me and all flesh that is on the earth" (Genesis 9:12-17).

Unfortunately, not much changed after the flood. Judgment did not change man's heart. Man was still corrupt, sinful, and disobedient. But even in the midst of sin, chaos, and rebellion, we continue to see God's faithfulness to his word and his plan.

TRACING THE COVENANTS—ABRAM

The book of Genesis can be arranged around the phrase "these are the generations of…" And, by tracing the genealogies, we are tracing the seed of the woman from Adam to Noah and from Noah to Abram and through all of Abraham's children. The promised seed will be the offspring of Eve, Adam, Noah, and Abram and his family.

God's covenant with Abram did not do away with his covenants with Adam and Eve, or with Noah. Rather, he built on them and gave us another glimpse of what redemption will look like. Out of all the peoples of the earth, God began the fulfillment of his plan first with one man (Noah), then with one family (Abraham, Isaac, and Jacob), then with one nation (Israel). But the scope of God's plan has always been the whole world.

When God called Abram to follow him, he said,

> Go from your country and your kindred and your father's house to the land that I will show you. And I will make of you a great nation, and I will bless you and make your name great, so that you will be a blessing. I will bless those who bless you, and him who dishonors you I will curse, and in you all the families of the earth shall be blessed (Genesis 12:1-3).

These three verses are filled with great promises. But what I want to focus on is the phrase "*so that* you will be a blessing" (emphasis added). The phrase "so that" is crucial. God was not giving up on the rest of the world. This was not about God and Abram only. God was calling Abram, setting him apart, and blessing him for a reason—so that through him, God would bless the whole world by keeping his covenant promises! God was still on his great rescue mission to redeem and restore his creation, and he was going to use Abram and his offspring to do that.

Remember that, from the beginning, God was on a mission to fill the whole world with his presence. That was true in Eden ("Be fruitful and multiply and fill the earth" Genesis 1:28). He wanted his people to bear his image and extend his kingdom. And we see that his heart had not changed because he continued with the same whole-earth mission with Abram.

God also promised Abram that he would give land to his offspring (Genesis 12:7). Throughout the rest of the story, we will call this the Promised Land because it was the land promised to Abram.

Before Craig and I moved to St. Louis to go to Covenant Seminary, we lived on what is arguably the most beautiful 15 acres in all of Kansas. I loved this land. I loved how my children could run, play, swim, and climb on this property. I loved how bright the stars were at night. I loved how I could ride my horse as fast as I wanted. There were times when I would sit outside and reflect on the fact that this piece of land had been in existence since the creation of the world—and I felt as if God had created it just for me, even though I knew he hadn't. I was to enjoy it only for a season, and then pass it on to others, just as it had been passed on to me. But I know what it is to be given a specific piece of land for a season.

Part of God's covenantal promises to his people involved giving them a specific piece of land for a season of time. It is in Genesis 12:1 that we get the first glimpse that land is going to be part of

God's plan. He tells Abram to go from his home to "the land that I will show you." God chose the land, and it is important to our understanding of God's mission to understand why. The land was given to locate God's children strategically in the world *so that* they could be a blessing to all the families of the earth. Canaan was perfectly situated for God's redemptive purposes. Michael Williams says,

> Why was Abraham promised the land of Canaan rather than some other piece of real estate? If God had chosen Abraham and Israel for some pampered and coddled existence in which the nation would relate only to him and not bear an active mission toward the rest of humankind, then Canaan was an exceedingly poor choice on God's part. But it was neither a mistake nor happenstance that Canaan, the crossroads of the ancient world, was chosen to be the dwelling place of Israel… God did not call his people to a mountain-top monastery but to a strip mall on Main Street.[3]

The same is true for us. God does not call us to live a pampered and coddled existence, but to live in light of the fact that we have been strategically placed. Wherever you are, you've been placed there by God's design—purposefully, intentionally. God's people are to be a blessing to the world. Abram was called, blessed, and promised a strategic location so that in him, "all the families of the earth" would be blessed. The same holds true for you and me.

TRACING THE COVENANTS—ABRAHAM

In chapter 2, we saw that God is the King over all creation, and his kingdom is the place where perfect justice, mercy, and righteousness rule. Although we long for such a place, there is not a country in the world that experiences perfect justice or completely righteous rule. As our hearts cry out for righteousness and peace, may we remember that only God executes those absolutely. There is not one person or platform that can offer perfect justice—save one. Only when the perfectly righteous and just King of kings is on his eternal throne and he establishes his kingdom rule over all the earth will that perfect justice be ushered in again. Only the perfect King can bring perfect justice. And, even as we work toward it now, we long for that day with eager expectation.

We should not be surprised, then, as we trace God's covenants, to see that the foreshadowing of a king comes early in the story. God told Abram, "No longer shall your name be called Abram, but your name shall be Abraham, for I have made you the father of a multitude of nations. I will make you exceedingly fruitful, and I will make you into nations, and kings shall come from you" (Genesis 17:5-6). Other kings will come first, but in anticipation of the one true King who can and will accomplish all of God's purposes.

The different aspects of God's covenant with Abraham can be found in Genesis 12, 15, and 17. But it is in Genesis 15 that we read of the traditional covenantal ceremony—the time when God literally "cut covenant" with Abraham. What's astounding about this covenant, however, is that instead of both God and Abraham making their way between the bloody and broken animals, we read that Abraham was asleep while God alone "passed between these pieces":

> Wherever you are, you've been placed there by God's design—purposefully, intentionally. God's people are to be a blessing to the world.

> [God] said to [Abraham], "Bring me a heifer three
> years old, a female goat three years old, a ram three
> years old, a turtledove, and a young pigeon." And he
> brought him all these, cut them in half, and laid each
> half over against the other. But he did not cut the birds
> in half…As the sun was going down, a deep sleep fell
> on Abram. And behold, dreadful and great darkness
> fell upon him…When the sun had gone down and
> it was dark, behold, a smoking fire pot and a flaming
> torch passed between these pieces. On that day the
> LORD made a covenant with Abram, saying, "To your
> offspring I give this land" (Genesis 15:9-10, 12, 17-18).

Theologically, most of us are comfortable with that. We fully affirm God's complete sovereignty—he does it all! And he does: he initiates, he moves toward us, he has a plan, and he accomplishes that plan. But did Abraham have a part to play? Did he have a responsibility to keep?

In other words, what was required of the man who was blessed so that the whole world would be blessed? The one to whom the land was promised, the one who would have kings and nations come from him? We read in Genesis 17, "When Abram was ninety-nine years old the LORD appeared to Abram and said to him, 'I am God Almighty; walk before me, and be blameless, that I may make my covenant between me and you, and may multiply you greatly'" (verses 1-2). Abraham was to be blameless. He was to be holy. Was he? Not perfectly, but more and more so as his life progressed.

This is a very important point to understand as we head into the rest of the Old Testament. Does God carry out his plan regardless of how people respond? Yes. God is ever faithful to his plan and his promises—but for the people to realize the blessing, they are required to walk in obedience. We know "the covenant always rests upon God's initiative and determination. God nevertheless places obligations upon man in covenant relationship...he calls his people to obey the word of God, walk in his ways, trust him, and lean upon his mercy."[4]

As we begin to talk about holiness, blamelessness, and obedience, it is so important to remember how we began this chapter. Are we to be blameless in order to earn our Father's love? No! He has set his love on us because that love compels him. Is the surety of his covenantal faithfulness based on our faithfulness or holiness? No! He is faithful in spite of our sin, and he is a covenant keeper even though we are covenant breakers. The call to holiness is a call of response. It is not so that we will earn God's love; it is because we have God's love. As we will see in the next chapter, we are God's children, and because he loves us, he wants us to behave accordingly.

Where do we fit into all of this? When you were little, did you ever sing "Father Abraham"? It is a song claiming that you and I are Abraham's children, and as you sing the song, you're supposed to move your arms and legs, turn around, and repeat the song over and over. I found the song confusing. How was I one of Abraham's sons, and why would that cause me to praise the Lord (to say nothing of moving my arms and legs in ways that had nothing to do with the song)? Well, the arm and leg movements still confuse me, but the lyrics now make sense.

In Genesis 17, God changed Abram's name to Abraham. *Abram* means "exalted father," and *Abraham* means "father of a multitude." The idea that he would be the father of many people and nations tied into the promise in Genesis 12:3 that "in you all the families of the earth shall be blessed." And in the New Testament, we read,

> It is not as though the word of God has failed. For not
> all who are descended from Israel belong to Israel, and

not all are children of Abraham because they are his
offspring, but "Through Isaac shall your offspring be
named." This means that it is not the children of the
flesh who are the children of God, but the children of
the promise are counted as offspring (Romans 9:6-8).

It is because we are the children of the promise, children of the
covenant, that we are Abraham's true children. We are heirs to the
promises made to Abraham, and we are to walk before the Lord
and be blameless too.

Points to Remember from Chapter 4

- It is God's love that compels him, not our obedience.
- Covenant is the binding promise of our King to be
  our God and to make us his people.
- God is a covenant-keeping God.
- God's sights have always been on the whole world.
- We are blessed so that we will be a blessing.
- As Abraham's descendants, we are also called to
  respond faithfully to the faithfulness of God.

Discussion Questions

1. Read Ephesians 1:3-8. What aspects of your adoption
   story do you see in these verses?

2. Read Jeremiah 30:22 and Ezekiel 36:28. When you think about the garden and all we lost because of sin, what does the repeated phrase mean to you?

3. Read Isaiah 54:8-10. What comfort do you receive from this passage, and why?

4. Have you ever thought of the Bible as the story of an unhappy father who constantly has to punish and rebuke his disobedient and naughty children? Or do you see the Bible as it is—the story of a most loving Father who consistently moves toward the sin and brokenness of his children in order to forgive and redeem them? What difference does that make?

5. Read Romans 4:11-12, 16-18. What is the promise based on? Who are counted as Abraham's children?

6. Read Deuteronomy 30:16-20. How does this help us understand the unfailing promises of God and, at the same time, the responsibility he places on his people to obey? What light does this shed on how God feels about holiness and obedience?

7. Read Psalm 119:1-11. What are some ways to walk blamelessly?

8. Read Zechariah 2:10-11. Who will join and be God's people? Why is that good news for us?

9. Either write below or share with your group one point, truth, or lesson that either challenged or encouraged you from this chapter.

For Further Study

1. Read Galatians 4:4-7. How do these verses tie together the heart of the Father, the rescue he provides, and the way we are to respond?

2. Read Genesis 9:1-7. Compare it with Genesis 1:26-30. What is the same? What is different?

3. Read Exodus 6:6-8. List the promises God made ("I will...").

4. Read John 14:15. What should our love compel us to do?

CHAPTER 5

A KINGDOM OF PRIESTS

Scripture Memory

"Now therefore, if you will indeed obey my voice and keep my covenant, you shall be my treasured possession among all peoples, for all the earth is mine; and you shall be to me a kingdom of priests and a holy nation" (Exodus 19:5-6).

Pray

"You are a chosen race, a royal priesthood, a holy nation, a people for his own possession, that you may proclaim the excellencies of him who called you out of darkness into his marvelous light" (1 Peter 2:9). Father, thank you for choosing me, calling me out of darkness, and making me your own. Help me to live in a way that proclaims your excellencies!

I grew up in a very moral home. The biblical standard of morality was the guide my parents used, but it was a morality that had very little to do with Jesus or with the story of redemption. It was a morality that screamed, "Good girls don't smoke, cuss, chew, or go out with boys who do." And, while part of me wanted to be a "good girl," most of the time, I tried to get my toes as close as I could to the line of lawbreaking without crossing it. I found all sorts of ways to skirt around the rules. For instance, we were not supposed to take the Lord's name in vain, so I would say "Ga" when I was upset. If my mom questioned me, I would respond, with indignation in my voice, "I said, 'Ga,'" and that seemed to satisfy her. My only motive for obeying my parents' rules was my desire to not be grounded. I viewed their rules as restrictions meant to kill my fun. The rules seemed outdated, boring, and irrelevant.

In the introduction to this book, I mentioned that Scripture is not a collection of dos and don'ts—and yet it contains lists of dos and don'ts. Consider the Ten Commandments. The majority start with the phrase "you shall not." You shall not steal, lie, murder, covet, or take the Lord's name in vain…but you shall honor your father and mother and remember the Sabbath. Isn't that just a list of dos and don'ts? What place do these rules have in our story? To answer these questions, we must examine when the Ten Commandments were given, and, more importantly, why they were given.

Let's review where we are in the story and what has happened up to this point. God created all that there is, and his creation was filled with peace, beauty, unhindered relationship with him, and unspeakable joy. Adam and Eve rebelled, sinned, and suffered the consequences. In spite of their sin, God pursued his children and promised to fix what they had broken, and to someday defeat their enemy permanently. God promised this victory would come through a man who would be a descendant of Adam, Noah, and Abraham. Then later, God communicated to Abraham two important points: God would bless Abraham so that, through him, all the families of the earth will be blessed; and, as part of that blessing, Abraham was to be blameless in his walk before God.

What happened next? Abraham had Isaac, Isaac had Jacob, Jacob had twelve sons, and they all ended up in Egypt (read Genesis 21–50 for all the details!). For 400 years, this family lived in Egypt, and they were fruitful and multiplied. They became not only a large family, but a large people group. The Egyptians felt threatened by this group, so they turned the descendants of Abraham into slaves.

But these people had been told about the God of their forefathers Abraham, Isaac, and Jacob, so they cried out to him to see if he would rescue them. And rescue them he did! He sent plagues, signs, and wonders to defeat the Pharaoh of Egypt, and he delivered his people from slavery and oppression. He then told them he was their God, and they were his people. And this is where we will now pick up the story.

THE PATTERN OF REDEMPTION

I recently finished reading a book that, when I reached the last page, I was amazed at how the author had woven so many pieces of the plot together. He had tied together all the different events and people in a way that was beautiful and astounding. As a result, by the end of the story, I could look back and identify which aspects of it had been the most important.

The second book of the Bible is Exodus, which means "departure" or "a going out," similar to our English word *exit*. And that is the major theme of the book—Israel's exit from Egypt. Why is an entire book of the Bible dedicated to this one event?

The exodus was an event that happened early in the storyline of God's great drama of redemption. But, by the time we get to the end of the story, we realize the exodus from Egypt was central to God's unfolding plan. It was not an isolated albeit wonderful incident that has little to do with us. Rather, the exodus was an event that foreshadows our glorious redemption and was the single greatest act of redemption apart from the cross. The exodus presents a model of what God's ultimate redemption would look like and is "repeatedly celebrated as the ground for Israel's hope and basis for God's future deliverances."[1] Read how Sandra Richter puts it:

> This [the exodus] is the single most important event in all Israelite history. Without the exodus, the children of Abraham were a forgotten race. Without the exodus, the promises of Abraham were nothing. Without the exodus, there would be no Mosaic covenant and no Israel...For all of history God has chosen to be identified by this singular event—the God who rescues slaves from their bondage and claims them as his own...If we are to understand the God of our salvation, the faith of Israel and therefore our own faith, we must understand the exodus.[2]

Exodus 2:24 says that God heard the groaning of his people and he "remembered his covenant with Abraham, with Isaac, and with Jacob." Therefore God, appearing in a burning bush, called a man named Moses and told him that he was going to use him to deliver his people from slavery. God sent Moses back to Pharaoh, and when the Egyptian king refused to let the Israelites go, God poured out the plagues. He turned water to blood; he sent locusts, frogs, gnats, flies, boils, and hail, to name a few. After the ninth plague, Pharaoh still refused to release the Israelites. As a result, God sent the tenth and worst plague.

The tenth plague is of utmost significance because it meant one of two things had to die—either a firstborn or a lamb. God warned Moses he was going to kill every firstborn in all of Egypt, whether Israelite or Egyptian. But if an Israelite family took a lamb without blemish, slaughtered it, and spread the blood on their doorframe, God would see the blood and pass over that house, sparing the firstborn.

> Tell all the congregation of Israel that on the tenth day of this month every man shall take a lamb according to their fathers' houses, a lamb for a household...Your lamb shall be without blemish, a male a year old. You may take it from the sheep or from the goats, and you shall keep it until the fourteenth day of this month, when the whole assembly of the congregation of Israel shall kill their lambs at twilight.

> Then they shall take some of the blood and put it on the two doorposts and the lintel of the houses in which they eat it...For I will pass through the land of Egypt that night, and I will strike all the firstborn in the land of Egypt, both man and beast; and on all the gods of Egypt I will execute judgments: I am the LORD. The blood shall be a sign for you, on the houses where you are. And when I see the blood, I will pass over you, and no plague will befall you to destroy you, when I strike the land of Egypt (Exodus 12:3, 5-7, 12-13).

This meant that, before the slaves were set free, either a firstborn child or a perfect lamb died. We'll get to this point of our story in a few more chapters. But Jesus was both the firstborn and the perfect lamb for us. Colossians 1:15 tells us the Jesus is "the first-born of all creation," and John 1:29 quotes what John the Baptist said when he saw Jesus: "Behold, the Lamb of God, who takes away the sin of the world!"

In Exodus, the slaves were set free because blood was shed. A group of people were delivered from oppression and slavery because either a firstborn son died, or a perfect lamb died. God was showing us the pattern of his redemption, and how high the cost of this rescue would be.

TREASURED POSSESSION

Did the exodus end when the Israelites crossed the Red Sea? Did they get to the other side, look around at each other, and ask, "Now what?" Was the whole point of their deliverance to simply get them out of Egypt? No. God wasn't only taking them *from* something; he was taking them *to* something.

To reference the Disney movie *Tangled* once again—when Rapunzel was rescued from the tower, did the audience stand up and leave, thinking the movie was over? No. Everyone knew Rapunzel's deliverance from the tower was an important and necessary step in the storyline, but it was not the final goal, which was for her to be reunited as a true daughter to the true king.

The Israelites were not delivered out of Egypt merely to be released from slavery. As Michael Williams says,

> The initial act of physical deliverance is just that, initial. More is to come. For all believers, salvation is more than deliverance from the oppression of sin, guilt, and death. God wants not only to save but also to enter into relationship with his covenant community and to bless that community. Relationship and blessing lie alongside deliverance at the heart of redemption.[3]

As we trace the main threads of the story through Scripture, we are trying to see what God is up to. And what we see is that he is fixing things for a reason. Because unless he does, he cannot be in relationship with his children. The goal of salvation is the restoration of relationship. God continues to desire what he had in the garden with Adam and Eve: He wants to be our God, he wants to be in relationship with us, he wants us to be his people, and he wants to dwell with us. So he redeems, rescues, and delivers— to bring us to himself.

After God brought all the former slaves out of Egypt, his first action was to bring them to the base of Mount Sinai and say,

> You yourselves have seen what I did to the Egyptians, and how I bore you on eagles' wings and brought you to myself. Now therefore, if you will indeed obey my voice and keep my covenant, you shall be my treasured possession among all peoples, for all the earth is mine; and you shall be to me a kingdom of priests and a holy nation. These are the words that you shall speak to the people of Israel (Exodus 19:4-6).

Do you see what God called the people? His treasured possession, a kingdom of priests, and a holy nation. What was their responsibility, or how were they to respond? Obey him and be faithful covenant keepers. As happened with all the other covenants. God initiated and provided. And God's people were to respond and obey.

The order of the events matters! What would have happened if the order had been reversed—if God had said to the people while they were still in Egypt, "If you obey my voice and keep my covenants, then I will bring you to myself and make you my treasured possession"? What would that have changed? Everything! In fact, all the other religions in the world are based on that order: If you do things right, then you will earn whatever it is that religion promises—nirvana, riches, enlightenment, etc. But that is not the order in Christianity.

> The goal of salvation is the restoration of relationship. God...wants to be our God, he wants to be in relationship with us, he wants us to be his people, and he wants to dwell with us.

God delivered his people because he loved them. He brought them to himself because he wanted to be in relationship with them. They were his treasured possessions; they belonged to him, and he delighted in them. They did nothing to earn any of this. The same is true for us. We are former slaves who have been rescued, delivered, and redeemed not because we earned it, but because God loves us. He loves you.

God's love is given before it is ever returned. He delivered you because he treasures you. And, because you don't earn it, neither can you lose it. Hallelujah, what a Deliverer!

KINGDOM OF PRIESTS AND A HOLY NATION

What did God mean when he told the people of Israel they were going to be a kingdom of priests? Did he mean they were going to walk around in white collars and black robes? No. To understand this phrase, it helps to consider what priests do. Priests act as a go-between, an intermediary between God and man. They talk to God about the needs and failures of the people, and they talk to the people about how to worship and serve God.

By calling the Israelites priests, God was telling them they were to serve the whole world by being go-betweens. They were to pray for the surrounding nations and tell them about their great and mighty God. He was inviting his people to be participants in his story. They now had a part to play in this great rescue mission— not only as receivers of God's mercy and grace, but also as those who could invite others in.

God united the Israelites to his mission to redeem a people for himself. As always, God's sights were set on the whole world. It might have been easy for this newly formed nation to think that when God said he wanted to be their God, he was rejecting the rest of the world. But that has never been the case. God's sights have always been on all the people of earth—even before the fall.

God was giving this new nation, Israel, not just a purpose, but also an identity: They were his people, treasured, loved, and redeemed. They had a mission: They were called to be both receivers of God's great mercy and extenders of it. Through them, God would make himself known throughout the world. And they were told what was required of them to be faithful partners in this beautiful relationship: They were to be holy. In other words, Israel was not saved for Israel's sake alone.

Peeking ahead in our story a bit, how well did Israel do at mediating God's presence and blessing to the surrounding nations? Not very! There were two big pitfalls the Israelites succumbed to as they tried to fulfill their calling: syncretism and separatism. *Syncretism* describes the merging of things (think of synthesis or synthetic—the combining of different things). And *separatism* is exactly what it sounds like—a removal or separation from those around you.

A large part of the Old Testament is the story of how the people of Israel insisted on synchronizing themselves with the surrounding nations. The book of Judges chronicles Israel's repeated downward spirals of leaving God, acting like the nations around them, being taken into captivity, crying out to God, and being rescued by God. Even many centuries later, in the book of Ezekiel, we read that Israel still wanted to "be like the nations" (Ezekiel 20:32).

The flip side of this coin is separatism. Even though syncretism was more often than not Israel's problem, at other times, Israel so far removed herself from engaging the other nations that she was completely ineffective in her call to minister to them. This was the problem Jesus addressed in the parable of the good Samaritan.

The priest and the Levite (both Israelite religious leaders) didn't stop to help the beaten man on the roadside because they didn't want to become "unclean." They were separatists.

Israel failed at fulfilling her mission to be a kingdom of priests to the world. But the good news is that we have one who did not fail; he was the perfect Israelite in every way. Kevin Vanhoozer says, "Part of what Jesus is accomplishing on the cross, then, is fulfilling the messianic vocation of Israel to be a faithful and obedient covenant people, a kingdom of prophets and priests, a light to the nations."[4] Jesus is the true and holy priest who can and does mediate God's blessings to the whole world, and the true King of the kingdom who now functions as God's light to a dark world.

REAL RELATIONSHIP

I like to play tennis. It is a fun game and a great outlet for my competitive nature. But tennis is no fun to play alone. To stand on a tennis court and hit the ball over a net and never have it returned is not tennis. Tennis requires at least two people so that the ball can go back and forth. Then it's fun! In the same way, relationships need people on each "side." Real relationship means that each party is present, willing to engage, and involved.

God constantly invites his people into real relationship with him—relationship that requires something from both sides. He is not the "great watchmaker" who set the world into motion and then stepped back to let it all play out. He is present, engaged, and involved. And we are not puppets, mere pawns in a game. Our responses and actions matter. We are called into real relationship. And that relationship comes with expectations and requirements.

That should not seem strange to us. What relationship doesn't come with expectations and requirements? Among the closest relationships I have are those with my children. My love for them is not tied, in any way, to their actions. I will love them no matter what they do and no matter what they don't do. But that love does not mean that our relationships don't have requirements and expectations. Even though my love for them cannot be broken, the closeness of my relationship with them can suffer heartache. When they were young, disrespect or unkindness on their part certainly caused distance between us—not in my love for them, but in the ways we related to each other. As adults, if they were to be uncommunicative or unloving, our relationships would be weakened, though my love wouldn't. We all know what it is like when a relationship that is close, joyful, and thriving becomes distant, strained, and frustrating. That can happen in our relationship with God.

The main difference is that God never fails on his side of the relationship. He never falls short. He is always present, engaged, involved, faithful, wise, and loving. He is the covenant-keeping God. We, on the other hand, fail, fall short, disobey, and grow distant. We are the relationship wreckers, the covenant breakers. But I am getting ahead of myself again. This is the place in the story where we learn not just about this relationship, but also what is required for it.

Think again about Exodus 19:5: "If you will indeed obey my voice and keep my covenant, you shall be my treasured possession." God is clear—he requires obedience.

We are not always comfortable with the "if-then" language in Scripture. It can sound as if God's actions are dependent on our actions. On the one hand, God can and will do all that is in his holy will to do. He will fulfill his promises and purposes. On the other hand, he requires covenant faithfulness on our part too. We get to participate in his plan. And God requires us to respond with faith and obedience.

Think about the Israelites: God did everything that was necessary to deliver them from Egypt. But at some point, the people had to stand up, walk out their front door, and march out of Egypt. They had to obey.

Consider Abraham: When he was 99 years old, God told him that he would have a son. Abraham believed him, but he still had to do something in response to that belief (or else Sarah would not have become pregnant). This was true about Noah: God chose him out of his own good and sovereign choice. But Noah had to pick up some gopher wood and start building a boat. It can be hard for us to figure out how God's complete sovereignty and our responsibility go together, but God has no trouble holding them together.

> We are called to real, living, active, and vibrant relationship with the Lord of all creation. Not to earn, secure, or sustain his love, but as the appropriate response to his love.

By the time of the exodus, God had already proven himself to be present, loving, and faithful. He had brought this large group of people out of Egypt, told them he loved them, and brought them to himself. He then told them what he expected of them. Again, remember, the requirements are not to earn his love, but are to be in response to his love. The Ten Commandments were the beginning of God's instructions on how he wanted his people to respond. They are not merely a list of dos and don'ts; they give God's people a proper way to respond.

We, too, are called to obedience. We, too, are called to keep the commands of the Lord. We are called to real, living, active, and vibrant relationship with the Lord of all creation. Not to earn, secure, or sustain his love, but as the appropriate response to his love.

THE LAW: IMAGE BEARING, FLOURISHING, AND WITNESSING

We started this chapter with the questions, Aren't the Ten Commandments just a list of dos and don'ts? And, what do they have to do with God's rescue mission? We have looked at Exodus 19:4-6 because, in order to understand the law of God, we must first understand that it was given to those he called his treasured possession and a kingdom of priests. It was given to people with whom he was in real relationship. And the order of events is crucial to our understanding of the law.

When I was a child, I thought God was similar to Santa Claus—someone watching from afar who is making a list and checking it twice. I was going to be found either naughty or nice. And I was pretty sure which list I would be on.

Then when I began to be curious about God in my early twenties, I was more like the rich young ruler in Mark 10:

> As he was setting out on his journey, a man ran up and knelt before him and asked him, "Good Teacher, what must I do to inherit eternal life?" And Jesus said to him, "Why do you call me good? No one is good except God alone. You know the commandments: 'Do not murder, Do not commit adultery, Do not steal, Do not bear false witness, Do not defraud, Honor your father and mother.' And he said to him, 'Teacher, all these I have kept from my youth'" (verses 17-20).

I thought to myself, *I've never murdered anyone, never committed adultery, never stolen anything...that I can think of.*

But was the law given to incite fear of the judge, to be a checklist for the naughty and nice, or to make the self-righteous feel better about themselves? No! At this point in the story, we should have two facts at the front of our minds. First, we should know that God loves his people and desires what is good for them—he loves to see his children flourish. God has never changed his mind about wanting the goodness of Eden for his children. Second, we should be firmly aware that God is on a mission to redeem a people for himself and has invited his children to participate in that mission. These two facts are our keys for understanding the law. The law was meant to help God's children flourish and to show others the goodness of being in God's family.

In our house, we had certain rules that our children were expected to obey. To name just a few, we didn't let them call each other names or hit each other; when they were small, they had to hold someone's hand when they crossed the street; they were required to look people in the eyes when speaking or being spoken to. When asked a question, they were expected to provide an answer. When called, they were to come. They were not allowed to interrupt. And the list could go on, but we had three reasons for these rules:

1. We wanted our family to be a safe place where each person flourished.

2. We wanted our children's actions to accurately reflect our family values.

3. We wanted to be a blessing to others.

God's law is not that different.

Our family's "laws" were not intended to be domineering or oppressive. As parents, we weren't trying to be killjoys. We didn't tell our children they couldn't play in the street because we wanted to ruin their fun. We told them that to promote their wellbeing; we wanted them safe from harm. Yes, the law—whether from parents or God—restricts at times, but only to promote the flourishing of those to whom the law applies.

The laws in our home were not just for us; we hoped to be a blessing to others. It's no fun to have a family over for dinner and have the kids throw food, hit each other, or call each other names. If that were to happen, nobody present would be blessed or want to come back.

Have you ever been around a family that loves and enjoys each other and treats one another with care and respect? Don't you want what they have, or to be a part of that? God's law had similar functions—to show a watching world what it looks like to be the people of the living God, and to make them want to be a part of that.

I had a professor who talked about "the floor and the ceiling" of the law. The floor, he said, was like the floor of a great cathedral. It is the place you enter and the platform on which you stand. But the ceiling is the place that lifts your eyes upward and can cause you to lose your breath in wonder and awe. In this sense, the Ten Commandments function as the floor. They serve as the bare minimum that we can do to reflect the character of God. If someone were to ask us about God, would we say, "My God is not a murderer, nor a liar, nor a thief, nor an adulterer. That is how great my God is"? No, that is the bare minimum—it is the floor. But the ceiling is the character of God himself: Instead of murder, he brings life; instead of lying, he is the source of truth; instead of stealing, he gives generously; and instead of adultery, he is ever faithful.

Exodus 34:5-7 offers a description of God's character: He is merciful, forgiving, loving, faithful.

> The LORD descended in the cloud and stood with him there, and proclaimed the name of the LORD. The

Lord passed before him and proclaimed, "The Lord, the Lord, a God merciful and gracious, slow to anger, and abounding in steadfast love and faithfulness, keeping steadfast love for thousands, forgiving iniquity and transgression and sin."

That is the ceiling—and the character God wants to inscribe on our hearts. In the same way that Craig and I had a bare minimum standard for our children—thou shall not hit each other—it was far from the best we had for them. We wanted them to love each other, serve each other, sacrifice for each other. But, at bare minimum, they were not to hit or call each other names. In a similar way, God provided the law to teach his children the bare minimum of how they should treat each other so there would be life and flourishing for all. The law is the floor of accurately bearing God's image; obedience and trust will be cultivated as we follow. And this prepares our hearts to strive for the ceiling—to "love the Lord your God with all your heart and with all your soul and with all your strength and with all your mind, and your neighbor as yourself" (Luke 10:27).

Points to Remember from Chapter 5

- The exodus is the pivotal event of the Old Testament because it set a pattern for God's redemption of people.

- God delivers people to bring them into relationship with himself.

- We, too, are slaves who have been rescued and redeemed.

- The goal of salvation is relationship and flourishing.

- Israel had a mission and a purpose—they were to be mediators of God's blessing to the whole world. Obedience matters. It is our side of covenant faithfulness.

- The law of God is for the flourishing of God's people.

Discussion Questions

1. All of us struggle at times with feeling like we have to earn God's love. List two or three ways we might try to "earn" God's love.

2. How is 1 Peter 2:9 a restating of Exodus 19:4-5?

3. Reflect for a moment on what it feels like to be called treasured and chosen. Our hearts long for both. Which words in Exodus 19:4-5 and 1 Peter 2:9 mean the most to you, and why?

4. Think of a time when you have either wanted to "fit in" with others, or you have felt drawn away from God by those around you. In what ways could that have been similar to the syncretism of the Israelites?

5. Skim over Deuteronomy 28 (especially verses 1-2 and 15). Describe what is happening in this scene.

6. Read Philippians 2:8. Describe the obedience of Jesus. In what ways does this inform or challenge your understanding about the importance of obedience in the life of a believer?

7. Read Exodus 20:1-17. What are some of the ways God is promoting life, safety, health, and flourishing in these laws?

8. Read Romans 7:12. What three words did Paul use to describe the law?

9. Either write below or share with your group one point,
   truth, or lesson that either challenged or encouraged
   you from this chapter.

For Further Study

1. Read Exodus 6:2-8. What is familiar in verse 7? In
   the chart below, list the seven "I will" statements God
   makes in verses 6-8. Then look up the verses in the
   second column and comment on how God has also
   done that for you.

Exodus 6:2-8		
I will...	Colossians 1:13	He has...
I will...	Romans 6:17-18	He has...
I will...	Ephesians 1:7	He has...
I will...	1 Peter 2:10	He has...
I will...	Revelation 21:3	He has...
I will...	John 14:2	He has...
I will...	John 14:3	He has...

2. Read Ephesians 2:8-9, 13. How do these verses reinforce what we have been talking about?

3. Read 1 John 4:16. Have you come to know and believe—*really* believe—that God loves you, and you are his treasured possession?

4. Read John 14:15, 24. How do we express our love to God? Describe what that looks like in your own life.

5. Read John 15:9-10. What connection is Jesus making? Which came first: the obedience or the love?

CHAPTER 6

A DWELLING PLACE FOR THE KING

Scripture Memory

"Your house and your kingdom shall be made sure forever before me. Your throne shall be established forever" (2 Samuel 7:16).

Pray

> *"Your throne, O God, is forever and ever. The scepter of your kingdom is a scepter of uprightness" (Psalm 45:6). Father, I praise you that you reign eternal. I praise you that your throne and your kingdom will never end. And I praise you that you are a good and righteous King!*

Our first child was born almost six weeks early. After a long and difficult labor, our son finally arrived. But he was in bad shape. Before I could see or hold him, he was whisked away to the neonatal intensive care unit. My thoughtful father-in-law, video camera in hand, went into the nursery and filmed a short video of him. My father-in-law then brought the camera and video to me in the recovery room. And that was how I first saw my son. That's not the way I had envisioned glimpsing my first child for the first time. Several hours went by before I was able to go see him, and even then, I couldn't hold him. He was in an incubator that separated us. I wanted to hold him but couldn't. His condition required that I keep some distance; in fact, his very life depended on it. So I sat as close to him as I could.

In some ways, this is the situation between our heavenly Father and his children. He longs to be with us. But we have a condition (unholiness) that makes it impossible for us to be in his presence. Our very lives are in danger because of this condition; the Holy cannot dwell in the midst of the unholy. What we see, though, is similar to the way I sat as close to the incubator as I could. God moves as close to his children as he can—he actually dwells among them.

We will see this first in the tabernacle and, eventually, in the temple. The freedom God had to walk with his children in the garden has been lost, but God makes a new way to draw near. He established for himself both a place to dwell and ways for his people to approach him. What we cannot lose sight of is the amazing love of our Father—and the lengths he goes to just to be near his children.

As a forewarning, this book is meant to be something like the beginning of a 500-piece puzzle, which enables you to put the edge pieces in place so that you can fill in the center later because you have the outline of the finished picture. In this chapter, we are going to skim through almost 1,500 years, picking up just a few more of the main pieces. We will look more closely at the heart of our Father, the tabernacle, the establishment of the kingdom, the temple, and the exile. Because these pieces are key to our understanding of the story. The center of the puzzle will begin to be filled in after the edges are put into place—I promise.

I WILL DWELL AMONG THEM

I love it when all my children are at home under one roof. I like being present in the kitchen while they are making coffee and talking, or sitting together with all of them around the table. I love the evenings when we can all sit on the back porch and simply be together. I enjoy playing board games with them or snuggling on the couch while we watch a movie together. I love being with my children.

Amazingly, God feels the same way! He loves to be with his children. We have looked at the heart of our Father—that he wants to be our God and wants us to be his people. But there is another very important (arguably the most important) piece to this picture we are putting together—a piece that was evident in the garden, and now becomes clear again.

God created Eden as a place where he could dwell with his people. Remember, they lived in such sweet closeness that Adam and Eve even knew the sound God's footsteps made (Genesis 3:8)! Can you even imagine such a sound? When he expelled them and placed the cherubim at the entrance to prohibit their return, the greatest loss of Eden was that of being able to dwell with God (and he with us) in such close intimacy.

As we've seen, the Holy cannot dwell with the unholy—that is the great dilemma portrayed in Scripture. God is holy; we are unholy. God is faithful; we are unfaithful. But he longs to be with his people, so he is working all things together to make it possible for us to dwell in his presence again. The presence of God with his people—dwelling together—is a theme that we need to trace from creation to glory to truly understand where this story is headed.

After Eden, we read of several accounts where God "occasionally descends to meet with selected individuals, although these encounters are always relatively brief and sometimes unexpected."[1] But when we come to the second half of Exodus, we read of a giant step forward in God's plan—the building of the tabernacle.

Starting in chapter 26 of Exodus, God gave the instructions for the building of the tabernacle. What's important to notice is that the tabernacle was God's idea, God's plan, and God's design. He established it for the purpose of dwelling in the midst of his people. In Exodus 29:45, we read, "I will dwell among the people of Israel and will be their God." The next verse tells us that this was the reason he brought them out of Egypt: "They shall know that I am the LORD their God, who brought them out of the land of Egypt that I might dwell among them. I am the LORD their God" (verse 46).

This is the heart of our Father, and it changes everything when we know that the God of the universe loves his people and wants to be with them. The love of our Father is what drives the story of redemption forward—God wanting to be our God and to dwell with us.

We all have a deep longing to be loved. Some of us have experienced being loved well, and some of us have not. It is worth taking a moment to stop here and soak in the fact that God says to his people, "I want to be in your midst. I want to be with you because I love you so deeply."

> The love of our Father is what drives the story of redemption forward—God wanting to be our God and to dwell with us.

How do we respond to such a love? Years ago, I was at a women's conference and had some time alone in my hotel room. I was praying and making my requests known to God. While praying, I realized that I was primarily seeking the provision and protection of the Lord. Seeking what his hand provides is good and right, but I was convicted that I needed to seek his face—to long for the very presence of the Lord, not just what he could do for me.

Psalm 27:7-8 says, "Hear, O Lᴏʀᴅ, when I cry aloud; be gracious to me and answer me! You have said, 'Seek my face.' My heart says to you, 'Your face, Lᴏʀᴅ, do I seek.'" In the same way that God told David to seek his face, God wants us to seek his face and presence because he loves to simply be with his children. Hence, the great dilemma: God longs to be with us and we desperately need to be with him, but our sinful, rebellious, and wayward hearts make it impossible to be in the unveiled presence of our holy God. We're doomed—unless God makes a way for us.

TABERNACLE

If we were to outline the book of Exodus, we would probably begin by breaking the book into two sections titled Egypt (chapters 1–18) and Sinai (chapters 19–40). The first half of the book begins with the plight of the people in Egypt and ends with them leaving Egypt. The second half, beginning in chapter 19, takes place at the base of Mount Sinai. It is here that the people were given the law and then instructions on how to build the tabernacle.

In any storyline, some moments are more important than others. In our story, the giving of the tabernacle is one of these key moments. God had created and called a people to himself. He had bound himself to them through his covenantal word. He had longed to dwell with them, and now, for the first time since Eden, God was going to reside with his people again. But this was not Eden. And we, the readers, know this as soon as God declared his desire to dwell among his people (Exodus 25:8) because he immediately gave them instructions, regulations, and laws concerning how to both build and approach the place where he would dwell. As Sandra Richter points out:

> The irony of the tabernacle is the agony of redemptive history. By its very form this structure communicates

God's desire for cohabitation. But the increasing restriction of persons—and the elaborate systems of sacrifice and mediation even for those approved persons—communicated the legacy of sin, separation.[2]

Even as God dwelt among his people, they were still separated by the simple fact that God is holy, and his people were not.

God used 13 chapters of Exodus to explain the rules and instructions for the construction of this new dwelling place, and then an entire book of the Bible, Leviticus, to give the guidelines for how to approach him in this place. Most of these were given for one of two reasons: to either remind them that he is holy, or protect them from that holiness because it's serious business for the unholy to dwell in the presence of the holy. The freedom of Eden had been lost, but the desire of the Father to be with his children was not.

The tabernacle, no matter how tent-like it looked, was far more than a mere tent in the desert. It was a palace for God, the high King of heaven. He took this lowly tent as his dwelling place. As Jay Sklar wrote, "The King (the Lord) dwelt in his earthly palace (the tabernacle) among his people (Israel)."[3] This should astound us.

God is the one who "sits above the circle of the earth" (Isaiah 40:22) and whose "glory [is] above the heavens!…who is seated on high, who looks far down on the heavens and the earth" (Psalm 113:5-6). And yet, God told his people to take wood and animal skins, cloth and metal, and make a tent for him.

Imagine how you would feel if Prince William and Princess Kate called to tell you they were going to move in with you. That, in and of itself, would be difficult to believe. But then, imagine they told you they would be staying in a tent in your backyard. That is incomprehensible; and yet what God did was even more so! The tabernacle was the place where the divine King chose to live.

Among the last words in the book of Exodus we read, "Then the cloud covered the tent of meeting, and the glory of the LORD filled the tabernacle" (40:34). God, the creator God, the God of all heaven and the whole earth, the God who defeated Pharaoh and delivered his people, was now dwelling in the midst of his people. And his glory filled the tabernacle. Of course it did! The glory of God is so great and so abundant that even the glory he chose to share with the Israelites would overflow and overwhelm them. God was still omnipresent (everywhere). He was still enthroned above the heavens and seated on high. The tabernacle did not contain him, for he is uncontainable. Of course the tabernacle was filled; nothing can contain the glory of the Lord.

Because a cloud settled on the tabernacle and God's glory filled it, not even Moses could go in (Exodus 40:35). God was already dwelling among his people, but they did not yet have full access. The phrase "already, but not yet" captures so much of our story. It means so much of this great story has already happened—and the end is a sure thing—but we do not yet live in the time of "happily ever after." Soon, but not yet. When God filled the tabernacle with his presence, an aspect of the "already, but not yet" tension was occurring. He was already dwelling with his people, but he was not yet fully approachable.

THRONE

You'll want to hold on, because we are now going to cover a lot of history in a short amount of time. In order to trace the threads of our story that hold it together, there will be times when we slow down to look intently at what happened in a period of a few short hours or days. At other times, we will skim over years and centuries of events and details. The fact we will be skimming through Scripture doesn't mean the events aren't important. They are, or

God wouldn't have chosen to put them in his inspired Word! But while some pieces of the story illuminate and add detail, others are the main thread of the storyline. So now, we are going to race through 400 years of history as we trace that thread!

As you know, the Israelites, after being delivered from slavery, were given an identity (treasured possession and kingdom of priests). They were given rules to obey (the law), showing them how they were to live as God's covenant children. Living this way was good for them and would enable them to accomplish God's purpose, which was to extend his kingdom by being a witness to the surrounding nations. And most importantly, God had ordained a way to fulfill the desire of his fatherly heart and dwell among his children (via the tabernacle and the sacrificial system). The Israelites were now ready to enter the land that had been promised to Abraham all those years ago.

But the people failed miserably. They did not live as a kingdom of priests. They did not uphold their side of covenant faithfulness. And they grieved the God who lived in their midst.

You probably know the story: The Lord brought them to the edge of the Promised Land, and they refused to go in (Numbers 13–14). As a result of their refusal to take what God had promised, God made them wander in the desert for 40 years. After that, the people finally entered the Promised Land, but they failed to completely conquer and occupy it (Judges 2:1-3). And as they lived in the land, they did not function as a kingdom of priests to the one true God. Rather, they worshipped the gods of the surrounding nations.

Earlier, we read about how the book of Judges shows Israel's repeated cycle of sin, slavery, supplication (crying out), and salvation. They continually bowed down to other gods and forsook their covenantal promises. Each time this happened, God allowed their enemies to overtake them. This would cause the Israelites to cry out for God's mercy and deliverance. God, ever faithful and mighty to save, would then send a deliverer and rescue them. Even so, the book of Judges ends with these sad words: "In those days there was no king in Israel. Everyone did what was right in his own eyes" (21:25).

There was no king in Israel. Really? Hadn't God gone out of his way to show the people he was their King? He had shown them he was the King of creation. He had shown them he was their covenantal King. The problem was not that the people didn't have a king; the problem was that they didn't acknowledge their King.

In his mercy, God gave Israel a human king. But that king was never meant to replace God; he was meant to represent God. God was still the King of all kings (including Israel's), and as we will see, he would take the new monarchy, weave it into his glorious plan of redemption, and "through the king...reveal some of the most glorious aspects of Israel's future."[4]

It is important to know what this appointed king was supposed to do. The king of Israel, like Adam and Eve, was to rule as a representative of the King. He was to rule in such a way that he promoted the law of God (righteous rule), caused the flourishing and well-being of the people, and served as a witness to God's kingdom to the surrounding nations.

The people chose the first king, Saul. He did not represent God, and God removed him from the throne. God chose the second king, David. It was with David that God established the next covenant. It was to David's reign that future kings were compared. And it was David's heart before the Lord that others were measured against. David was the king who established Jerusalem as the capital city of Israel. He brought the ark and the tabernacle into Jerusalem and, in doing so, brought "the throne room of the true king of Israel"[5] there.

Under David's rule, the promises to Abraham became realities. Christopher Wright says, "With David the covenant with Abraham had come to a measure of fulfillment: Abraham's offspring had become a great nation; they had taken possession of the land promised to Abraham; they were living in a special relationship of blessing and protection under Yahweh."[6] As promised, kings and nations had come from Abraham.

Israel was ready, finally, to function as the kingdom of priests the nation had been called to be. So David, the man after God's own heart, decided it was time to build a permanent palace for the rightful King. But God had other plans and said to David,

> When your days are fulfilled and you lie down with your fathers, I will raise up your offspring after you, who shall come from your body, and I will establish his kingdom. He shall build a house for my name, and I will establish the throne of his kingdom forever...And your house and your kingdom shall be made sure forever before me. Your throne shall be established forever (2 Samuel 7:12-13, 16).

Once again, God entered a covenantal promise with his people through a single person, a representative. But there was something new in this covenant—an eternal kingdom with an eternal throne. What must David have thought? What must the people of Israel have thought?

David's son, Solomon, became king after David. The Israelites might, at first, have thought that Solomon was the one promised in the covenant. He was David's son. He succeeded David, he built the temple, and he had a wise and righteous rule—at least in the beginning. But was his throne established forever? No. Almost immediately upon Solomon's death, the kingdom of Israel was divided into two—the northern and southern kingdoms. And it remained divided until after the exile.

So, who was the one who would sit on this eternal throne? If not David or Solomon, who? God's people looked year after year for the answer to that question. Throughout the rest of Israel's history, we see the people looking for the one, longing for this covenant to be fulfilled, longing for a Davidic king, someone who would finally sit on the promised eternal throne.

The Israelites were looking for another king, one like David, chosen and anointed by God, one whose rule was good and righteous—a king under whom the people would flourish and the kingdom would be extended. How would this happen? "How could Yahweh fulfill such a tall order? The answer, of course, will be by means of an offspring of David who will reach beyond David and Israel and is himself eternal."[7] They had a name for this person— the Messiah. And all of Israel was looking for him.

TEMPLE

David was on the throne. The ark of the covenant and the tabernacle were in Jerusalem (2 Samuel 6; 1 Chronicles 6:31-32). David had a palace and peace on all sides, but he wanted more. He didn't want God living in a tent that could be moved. He wanted God to be permanently fixed in Jerusalem. David knew that God's people were no longer wanderers but were now settled. The "lowercase *k*" king had a permanent home, and David wanted the "uppercase *K*" King to have one too. He asked God if he could build a house for him, but God told David no. David had shed too much blood, so David's son, Solomon, would be the one to build this glorious palace for the King (2 Samuel 7:1-17). David obeyed, and passed the plans for the temple on to Solomon.

The book of 1 Kings begins with David passing the throne on to Solomon, and one of the first acts of the new king was to start the construction of the temple. The temple was to replace the tabernacle; what had been a moveable tent was to now be a permanent palace. But the purposes of the two were the same— to be the place where God would dwell among and meet with his people.

After the temple was finished, we read about a repeat of what happened at the end of the book of Exodus: "the glory of the LORD filled the house of the LORD" (1 Kings 8:11). As we read 1 Kings 8:1-11, we should sigh with contentment. Isn't this it? Isn't this where the story has been headed since Adam and Eve were exiled from Eden? At this moment in Israel's history, a seed of Adam, Noah, Abraham, and David was king. He was a wise, just, and (mostly) righteous king. He was seated on David's throne. The people of Israel were living in the Promised Land. The temple had been built, and the presence of the Lord had filled the temple. The people were set to be a kingdom of priests and a blessing to the rest of the world as they lived according to the ways and words of the Lord, their true King. This is the high point in Israel's history!

Unfortunately, this scenario didn't last long. But, then again, it wasn't meant to. As good as this was, we were created for more. We were created for more than a mostly good king; we were created for a perfect King. We were created for more than a small strip of land along the Mediterranean; we were created to rule the whole earth. We were created for more than meeting with our God through a veil and a priest; we were created to walk with him and see him face to face.

First Kings begins with the death of David, and 2 Kings ends with the exile of the last Davidic king. The books begin with the construction of the temple and end with the destruction of the temple. The books begin with a united kingdom living under David's rule and end with a kingdom divided into two, with both taken into exile. If the people in 1 Kings 8:11 thought that they "had it made," their joy and hope didn't last long.

The books of 1 and 2 Kings chronicle the history of Israel from the end of David's reign until the Israelites are taken into exile. Immediately after Solomon's reign, the kingdom split in two—the northern kingdom (Israel) and the southern (Judah). Every subsequent king in both the northern and southern kingdoms is mentioned and evaluated in these books.

If we were to read all 47 chapters of 1 and 2 Kings, we would discover that the northern and southern kingdoms had a combined total of 39 kings. None of the kings in the northern kingdom were considered

> We were created for more than meeting with our God through a veil and a priest; we were created to walk with him and see him face to face.

good, and only four of the kings in the southern kingdom were. They either did (the four) or did not (the other 35) walk in the ways of the Lord. That is the standard by which God assessed their reigns. It is no wonder that God, after 400 years of the people not walking with him and not obeying all that he had said, sent them into exile. They lost the land, their king, and, most of all, the temple—because they had disobeyed and grieved the heart of their God.

EXILE AND RETURN

Were you ever grounded as a child? And sent to your room? I

was. A lot. I spent many an hour on my bed, and was supposed to think about what I had done wrong, what I would do differently in the future, and how I was to make amends. Sometimes I would do that, but usually I read a book or spent time daydreaming about riding horses or playing with friends. My time-outs didn't always serve the purpose for which they were given.

I do, however, remember what I felt like when the time-outs were over. I was, of course, glad for my time of punishment to end. But it was hard to go talk with my mom. I knew I had done wrong. I knew I had disobeyed, offended, and hurt her. A more tenderhearted child might have wanted to run back into her arms, apologize, and restore the relationship. But I rarely felt like that. Even as a child, I had a hard time admitting when I was wrong. Yes, my heart longed for restoration, but the combination of my pride and shame kept me from seeking restoration.

The Israelites were sent into a type of time-out, known as the exile. The northern kingdom was taken first, by the Assyrians, in 722 BC. The southern kingdom was taken into exile approximately 135 years later, in 587 BC, by the Babylonians. As we have seen, God's people had been disobedient and disloyal. God had been patient with them. He had warned them, over and over and over again. When the kings were not walking with the Lord, God sent prophets to talk to them, to remind and rebuke them. He sent man after man: Jonah, Joel, Amos, Hosea, Isaiah, Micah, Nahum, Zephaniah, Habakkuk, Jeremiah, Obadiah, and Ezekiel. But nothing worked.

When my kids were little, Chuck E. Cheese was at the top of my list of favorite places to hang out. A group of us—about ten women—went every other Thursday after Bible study. We would check in, order pizza, and sit and talk for hours as our kids ran around screaming and having fun. When it was time to leave, you would think that our children would have been happy, content, grateful, and obedient. But they were the opposite! They would whine, cry, and throw a fit.

On a good day, I would not tolerate my children's disobedience. But on a bad day, when I was exhausted, I did what every other mom finds herself doing at times: I would tell them to put on their shoes; they would ignore me and keep running around. I would tell them to sit down; they would ignore me and keep running around. I would tell them what to do, tell them again, threaten them, and count to three. (Now, I would love to branch into parenting advice here and tell all of you young moms not to do this, but that ruins the point I am trying to make.) The point is, no amount of goodness shown to my children would compel them to obey, and no amount of instruction or threats had any effect. Two things caused them to obey: discipline and a change of heart.

That is what the people of God needed too. They needed to be disciplined, and they needed a change of heart. First came the discipline.

We read in 2 Kings 18:11-12:

> The king of Assyria carried the Israelites away to Assyria and put them in Halah, and on the Habor, the river of Gozan, and in the cities of the Medes, because they did not obey the voice of the LORD their God but transgressed his covenant, even all that Moses the servant of the LORD commanded. They neither listened nor obeyed.

And in 2 Kings 25:20-21:

> Nebuzaradan the captain of the guard took them and brought them to the king of Babylon at Riblah. And

the king of Babylon struck them down and put them
to death at Riblah in the land of Hamath. So Judah
was taken into exile out of its land.

The people in both the northern and southern kingdoms were
taken into exile.

In case you are tempted to think that the Old Testament words
and commands of God are not relevant to us today because they
were given so long ago, I would encourage you to consider the gravity
of the verses above. The punishment Israel and Judah received was
due to the fact the people had "transgressed his covenant" and neither "listened [to] nor obeyed" the words and commands that God
had given to Moses at least 500 years before. But God did not leave
them without hope. He told the people in exile why they were in
exile—they had not listened to nor obeyed his Word.

The Israelites knew they were being punished because they
didn't keep the Word of the Lord. Had they thought it was irrelevant and outdated? If they had, they learned they were wrong—
the Word of God will stand forever. The same is true for us. God
is the same yesterday, today, and forever, and his Word stands for
all time.

Back to what happened at Chuck E. Cheese—until my children had a change of heart, my rebukes and reminders seemed
to bear no fruit of obedience. But discipline did, so I disciplined
them. In a similar way, after almost 500 years of rebukes and
reminders given through numerous prophets, the people of God
were still disobedient and disloyal. So God punished them and
sent them into exile.

Now, let's think back to an earlier time in the story, when
God exiled his people and cast them out of their land in Genesis
3. Was punishment God's final answer to sin for Adam and Eve?

No! Redemption was. Punishment was for the purpose of redemption. The same is true for Israel.

The people of God were sent into exile. The discipline occurred, but did it change the hearts of the people? Not really. So God spoke through the prophet Ezekiel and promised that a new covenant was coming—a covenant that would do what the others before had not been able to do:

> I will take you from the nations and gather you from all the countries and bring you into your own land. I will sprinkle clean water on you, and you shall be clean from all your uncleannesses, and from all your idols I will cleanse you. And I will give you a new heart, and a new spirit I will put within you. And I will remove the heart of stone from your flesh and give you a heart of flesh. And I will put my Spirit within you, and cause you to walk in my statutes and be careful to obey my rules. You shall dwell in the land that I gave to your fathers, and you shall be my people, and I will be your God (Ezekiel 36:24-28).

God said he would remedy the problem of both their unholiness and their unfaithfulness! He would give them new hearts that would enable and cause them to obey him. The questions to ask now are *when* and *how*: When will this glorious promise come to fruition, and how could this possibly be? Just wait—the answer is glorious!

Points to Remember from Chapter 6

- God wants to dwell with his people, but the great dilemma, as explained in Scripture, is that the unholy cannot dwell with the holy.

- Our sin keeps us from being able to dwell with a holy God, and keeps us from flourishing in the way he desires for us to.

- We were created for the perfect King and a right relationship with God.

- Punishment is not God's final answer to sin. Redemption is.

- The new covenant promises new hearts that can obey God.

Discussion Questions

1. Read Psalm 27:4-8. What one thing did David's heart long for, and what did the Lord tell David to seek? Ultimately, we will all seek that which our heart most longs for. What do you long for? How do you seek it?

2. Read John 14:2-3. How is our greatest hope also the fulfillment of our Father's desire to be with us? Do you believe the sure promise of John 14:3? Why or why not?

3. What would it have meant to the Israelites to have
   God's very presence in their midst? Does knowing that
   your heavenly Father wants to be with you change
   how you spend time with him in prayer? How and
   why?

4. The people of Israel were sent into exile because their
   hearts were led astray, and they did not obey God.
   What about you? What are some ways that you've
   grieved the heart of God? Why would you want to
   avoid causing God such grief?

5. With what attitude should we approach God? In what
   ways should our attitude be informed by the fact that
   God is a holy God, and that he is a loving Father who
   longs to dwell with us?

6. In the book of Judges, we saw Israel's repeated cycle of sin, slavery, supplication, and salvation. Have you ever felt caught in this same cycle? Why do we tend to cry out only in times of trouble?

7. From what do you currently need God to deliver you?

8. How does the promise of new heart, a heart that can obey God, encourage you, and why?

9. Either write below or share with your group one truth, point, or lesson that either challenged or encouraged you from this chapter.

For Further Study

1. Read Exodus 26:31-33. What is commanded? Why? How is this a reminder of God's holiness? How is this a protection for God's people and a display of God's mercy?

2. Read Psalm 89:3-4, 20-37. Who do you think the psalmist is talking about? Why? List any New Testament references that support your answer.

3. Read 1 Kings 6:1. To what event is the building of the temple tied? Why do you think this is?

4. Skim 1 Kings 8:12-61. This is Solomon's prayer to the Lord after the temple was built. What did Solomon say in verse 60 about the purpose of the presence of the Lord with his people? Where have you heard this before? In what ways does the Lord's presence in your life let "all the peoples of the earth…know that the LORD is God"?

5. Read Ezra 6:13-18. Compare the dedication of the temple built after the exiles returned to the dedication of Solomon's temple in 1 Kings 8:1-11. What important event is missing in Ezra? What glorious promise is given in 1 Kings 8:27?

CHAPTER 7

THE HERO ARRIVES

Scripture Memory

"Behold, the virgin shall conceive and bear a son, and they shall call his name Immanuel (which means, God with us)" (Matthew 1:23).

Pray

"An angel of the Lord appeared to them, and the glory of the Lord shone around them, and they were filled with great fear. And the angel said to them, 'Fear not, for behold, I bring you good news of great joy that will be for all the people. For unto you is born this day in the city of David a Savior, who is Christ the Lord. And this will be a sign for you: you will find a baby wrapped in swaddling cloths and lying in a manger.' And suddenly there was with the angel a multitude of the heavenly host praising God and saying, 'Glory to God in the highest, and on earth peace among those with whom he is pleased!'" (Luke 2:9-14). Thank you, Lord, for sending us your Son— the Savior of the world. Glory to God in the highest, indeed!

Waiting. Silence. Expectation. Silence. Hope. Silence. For 400 years after their return from exile, the people of God waited with no word from God. They returned to the Promised Land. They rebuilt Jerusalem and the temple—but neither was as glorious as it had been. And the people waited, and wondered. Where were the prophets? There were none. Where was their king? There wasn't one. Where was their God? He, too, was waiting... until just the right time.

In a quiet little town in northwest Israel, the 400-year silence was broken with this announcement: "Behold, the virgin shall conceive and bear a son, and they shall call his name Immanuel (which means, God with us)" (Matthew 1:23). Whatever or whomever the people thought they were waiting for, this was more—it was more than they ever thought to hope for. *God* with us. God *with* us. God with *us*!

In the story of God's redemptive plan, we have come to that glorious moment when, if this were a movie, the scene would grow quiet and there would be intense anticipation in the silence. Then the music would begin to soar as the hero came onto the screen. The time of waiting is over; the hero has arrived! Are you feeling a crescendo of music in your soul right now? You should be. Are you hearing trumpets blare as the great King rushes over the horizon? You should be. He has arrived! He is Immanuel, God with us.

> An angel of the Lord appeared to them, and the glory of the Lord shone around them, and they were filled with great fear. And the angel said to them, "Fear not, for behold, I bring you good news of great joy that will be for all the people. For unto you is born this day in the city of David a Savior, who is Christ the Lord. And this will be a sign for you: you will find a baby wrapped in swaddling cloths and lying in a manger." And suddenly there was with the angel a multitude of the heavenly host praising God and saying, "Glory to God in the highest, and on earth peace among those with whom he is pleased!" (Luke 2:9-14).

Yes, glory to God in the highest! God didn't stand at a distance, shouting instructions about how we could save ourselves. He didn't send a trusted advisor or angelic ambassador. Rather, he sent his own beloved Son, who took on flesh to dwell among us. Jesus came to save us. And it is vitally important to know *how* he saves us.

If I were to tell you we are saved by works, you would probably shut this book and never open it again. And, yet, in the truest sense, we are saved by works…but hold on before you close this book! The works that save us are not *our* works, but Jesus's. He did what was necessary to save us. He lived a sinless and perfectly obedient life, and then offered all the benefits of that sinless, perfect life to us. He received the punishment for our sin—he was beaten, mocked, flogged, spit upon, and crucified. On our behalf, Jesus died the death we deserved. And he was raised so we would be too. These are the works that save us—not ours, but his.

In order to understand how Jesus's works save us, one theologian explains, "Scripture interprets Christ's saving work by painting pictures. It uses images, motifs, themes to explain what Jesus did for us."[1] We're going to look at five of the pictures that the Bible gives us: Jesus as our second Adam, our Reconciler, our Redeemer, our Perfect Sacrifice, and our Champion. Each picture will help us to better understand different aspects of the one salvation Jesus accomplished.

JESUS THE SECOND ADAM

We live with brokenness every day. It's always around us and in us. In fact, we've never known a time when it wasn't this way. We have become so used to brokenness we forget it's there. We think this is normal. Until something happens that strikes the core of our soul, and we are reminded this isn't the way life is supposed to be. We are surrounded by brokenness but have been created for wholeness.

When something is broken, we want it fixed. When an appliance is broken, we wait impatiently for the repairman to come. When an arm is broken, we rush to the emergency room for medical help. We don't like living with broken things—marriages, friendships, equipment, policies, people. Brokenness makes us long for things to be unbroken, and that time of longing and waiting can be hard.

We've already seen that the people of Israel had been waiting. And waiting. And waiting. But it wasn't just the people of Israel, and it wasn't just for 400 years. Ever since Eve's teeth sank into that piece of fruit, all of creation has been waiting for the brokenness that followed that one act of disobedience to be fixed. Ever since God spoke the words in Genesis 3:15, all of creation has been watching and waiting to see when, and where, and how that promise would be fulfilled. When would a seed of the woman crush the head of their enemy? When would a man be sent who would (and *could*) be the champion they needed?[2] When would God make all things right again?

In his perfect timing, God sent one to *do* what Adam and Eve should have done—obey God perfectly—and by doing so, undo the results of the curse. Where every other person failed, Jesus succeeded; where every other disobeyed, Jesus obeyed; where every other fell short, Jesus overcame. Jesus was sent to fix the brokenness.

In Luke's Gospel, the genealogy of Jesus is carefully presented in chapter 3. It ends with Jesus, "the son of Adam, the son of God" (verse 38). Immediately afterward, in Luke 4, Jesus is sent into the wilderness to be tempted by the devil. As Robert Peterson points out, "The first Adam was tested by Satan in the beautiful Garden of Eden with one test and failed. The second Adam was tested by Satan in the wilderness with three tests and passed."[3] Luke was showing his reader that Jesus, the son of God and the son of Adam, is not only the offspring promised in Genesis 3, he is the *second* Adam. He was the one sent to redo and, therefore, undo what happened in the garden. Where Adam was disobedient, Jesus was obedient. Where Adam failed, Jesus succeeded.

> It was Jesus's obedience that led him to the cross, where he died the death that we should have died. Adam's disobedience brought us death; Christ's obedience brings us life.

Philippians 2:8 tells us that Jesus, "being found in human form…humbled himself by becoming *obedient* to the point of death, even death on a cross" (emphasis added). Our salvation is accomplished through the obedience of Christ. Not only are his perfect obedience and righteousness imputed (credited) to us, but it was also Jesus's obedience that led him to the cross, where he died the death that we should have died. Adam's disobedience brought us death; Christ's obedience brings us life.

Romans 5:12-19 beautifully lays out the vast differences between the two Adams:

> Just as sin came into the world through one man, and death through sin, and so death spread to all men because all sinned—for sin indeed was in the world before the law was given, but sin is not counted where there is no law. Yet death reigned from Adam to Moses, even over those whose sinning was not like the transgression of Adam, who was a type of the one who was to come.
>
> But the free gift is not like the trespass. For if many died

through one man's trespass, much more have the grace of God and the free gift by the grace of that one man Jesus Christ abounded for many. And the free gift is not like the result of that one man's sin. For the judgment following one trespass brought condemnation, but the free gift following many trespasses brought justification. For if, because of one man's trespass, death reigned through that one man, much more will those who receive the abundance of grace and the free gift of righteousness reign in life through the one man Jesus Christ.

Therefore, as one trespass led to condemnation for all men, so one act of righteousness leads to justification and life for all men. For as by the one man's disobedience the many were made sinners, so by the one man's obedience the many will be made righteous.

Peterson comments on these verses, saying, "The first Adam brought sin and death, the second Adam grace and life. The first Adam brought condemnation, the second Adam justification. The first Adam brought the reign of death, the second Adam the reign of life."[4] And this is great news! But the question we should all be asking is, How do I receive the grace, the life, and the justification the second Adam accomplished?

First Corinthians 15:21-22 tells us: "For as by a man came death, by a man has come also the resurrection of the dead. For as *in* Adam all die, so also *in* Christ shall all be made alive" (emphasis added). That's the answer: We must be *in* Christ. But how? This is the single most important question a person will ever ask. Literally, it is a question of life and death—life for those who are in Christ, and death for those who remain in Adam. *How can I find myself "in Christ"?*

According to Jesus, we must be born again:

> Now there was a man of the Pharisees named Nico-
> demus, a ruler of the Jews. This man came to Jesus by
> night and said to him, "Rabbi, we know that you are a
> teacher come from God, for no one can do these signs
> that you do unless God is with him." Jesus answered
> him, "Truly, truly, I say to you, unless one is born again
> he cannot see the kingdom of God." Nicodemus said
> to him, "How can a man be born when he is old? Can
> he enter a second time into his mother's womb and
> be born?" Jesus answered, "Truly, truly, I say to you,
> unless one is born of water and the Spirit, he cannot
> enter the kingdom of God. That which is born of the
> flesh is flesh, and that which is born of the Spirit is
> spirit. Do not marvel that I said to you, 'You must be
> born again'" (John 3:1-7).

Jesus ended this conversation with the words, "Whoever believes
in [the Son of Man] may have eternal life" (verse 15).

We are all born physically as sons and daughters of the first
Adam. We must be born *again*, spiritually, as a son or daughter of
God. That new birth takes place when you look to Jesus and "confess with your mouth that Jesus is Lord and believe in your heart
that God raised him from the dead, you will be saved" (Romans
10:9). At that point, a person is born again spiritually. And that
new birth happens only through Jesus, the second Adam. We are
then united to him for all eternity. This is what Scripture calls
being *in Christ*.

The reason I said this is the single most important question any
person will ever answer is because, like Paul said in 1 Corinthians
15:22, "As in Adam all die, so also in Christ shall all be made alive."
Are you still in Adam, or have you been born again through the

works of the second Adam? Our eternal destiny is determined by which Adam we are in.

JESUS THE RECONCILER

There are two aspects to reconciliation: First, a *disruption* in a relationship, and second, a *restoration* of that same relationship. Our relationship with our heavenly Father was once good and right (Genesis 1–2), but this relationship was broken. Reconciliation is the act that brings the Father and his children back together—and the Reconciler is the one who accomplished the reconciliation.

You'll remember, in the previous chapter, we saw that God longs to dwell with his children again, like he did in Eden. But our sin has disrupted that relationship. Ever since Eden, we have been, at best, alienated from our Father. But Scripture tells us our situation is even worse than that.

Romans 5:10 says that "if, when we were enemies, we were reconciled to God by the death of his Son, much more, being reconciled, we shall be saved by his life." Did you notice what God called us? Enemies! Not beloved children. Not cute little people who sometimes frustrate God. Prior to being reconciled, we were God's *enemies*. And our reconciliation was accomplished—look at the verse again—by the death of God's own Son. God sent his beloved Son to die for his enemies. Our reconciliation was unfathomably costly.

But God wanted to be reconciled with us! He was the one who initiated and accomplished this, the greatest act of love imaginable. And, as soon as we're reconciled with God through faith in his Son, we are given one of the sweetest gifts of our salvation—peace: "Since we have been justified by faith, we have peace with God through our Lord Jesus Christ" (Romans 5:1).

And don't we all long for peace! Peace is what ensues when a broken relationship is restored, and this is what the Reconciler offers us—peace with our Creator. It is a deep peace, a lasting peace, and a secure peace because it rests on the finished work of Christ. We are all familiar with types of peace that are fragile—treaties that are broken, friendships and marriages that dissolve—but this peace is not like that. Peace with God is one of the first, sweet fruits of our salvation. Have you ever heard someone tell of their conversion experience? Many people say, "I felt an immediate peace wash over me." It's a peace that we can sit in, rest in, and live in.

However, this peace is not just for us to receive. We are called to share about it. After we have been reconciled, God calls us to tell others that reconciliation and peace are possible. We are to implore others to be reconciled to God:

> If anyone is in Christ, he is a new creation. The old has passed away; behold, the new has come. All this is from God, who through Christ reconciled us to himself and gave us the ministry of reconciliation; that is, in Christ God was reconciling the world to himself, not counting their trespasses against them, and entrusting to us the message of reconciliation. Therefore, we are ambassadors for Christ, God making his appeal through us. We implore you on behalf of Christ, be reconciled to God. For our sake he made him to be sin who knew no sin, so that in him we might become the righteousness of God (2 Corinthians 5:17-21).

If you have been reconciled to God through the life, death, and resurrection of his Son, then you have been given the ministry of reconciliation. Our task is to beseech others to be reconciled with

God. And we do this through both our words (what we say) and our deeds (what we do).

With our words, we tell others of our reconciliation with God. We tell them that Jesus died so that we could be God's child instead of his enemy. And we must also show people the fruit of that reconciliation through our deeds. Part of being reconciled to God means living out that reconciliation with those around us.

Is there anyone in your life with whom you need to be reconciled? If you've been reconciled to God, let that great reconciliation compel you to pursue reconciliation with those who have hurt you and those with whom relationship has been broken. But because we live in a world that is still broken, we all know that reconciliation is not always possible. Paul helpfully wrote, "If possible, as far as it depends on you, live at peace with everyone" (Romans 12:18 CSB). If possible. Aren't you glad he put that in there? There will be people with whom, on this side of glory, it is not possible to be reconciled. But we need to pursue reconciliation "as far as it depends on [us]."

We also need to remember that when the Bible talks about reconciliation, it doesn't refer only to what happens between God and man, or even between one individual and another. Reconciliation can also take place between groups of people. In Ephesians, Paul wrote,

> Remember that at one time you Gentiles in the flesh, called "the uncircumcision" by what is called the circumcision, which is made in the flesh by hands— remember that you were at that time separated from Christ, alienated from the commonwealth of Israel and strangers to the covenants of promise, having no hope and without God in the world. But now in Christ Jesus you who once were far off have been brought near by

the blood of Christ. For he himself is our peace, who
has made us both one and has broken down in his flesh
the dividing wall of hostility (2:11-14).

The division Paul was addressing was between Jew and Gentile.
They were divided along lines of ethnicity and nationality. But Jesus
tore that dividing wall down "in his flesh." Through Christ, God
is making one group of people for himself, and this one group of
people—made from every tribe, tongue, and nation—is to love,
serve, honor, pray, rejoice, and live in harmony with one another.
We have been reconciled to God, and we are now to be reconciled
to each other. One day, when all that is broken has been made right,
we will be one group, surrounding one throne, singing one song,
with one voice, to one King, who is on his one throne (Revelation
7:9). That future reality is meant to break into our current life and
create the beautiful, visible fruit of reconciliation that all the world
can see. Do you live as a reconciled person?

JESUS THE REDEEMER

Fanny Crosby rejoiced in redemption when she wrote:

> Redeemed, redeemed,
> Redeemed by the blood of the Lamb;
> Redeemed, redeemed,
> His child, and forever, I am.[5]

You can probably think of many other hymns and worship songs
that highlight Jesus as our Redeemer. We often lift our hands and
our voices to sing about our redemption. But what does it mean
to be redeemed?

When a person is taken captive, sometimes their captors will
demand a ransom. This is the price paid in exchange for that
person's freedom, for their redemption from captivity. When the

demand of a ransom is met and the exchange occurs, we say the person has been redeemed. The ransom is the cost of redemption—and Jesus is both our Ransom and our Redeemer.

Jesus, quoting from Isaiah 61, said, "The Spirit of the Lord is upon me, because he has anointed me to proclaim good news to the poor. He has sent me to proclaim liberty to the captives and recovering of sight to the blind, to set at liberty those who are oppressed" (Luke 4:18). Jesus came to set captives free. And Scripture is clear that we are all born as slaves to sin (John 8:34; Romans 6:6). We are held captive by the law because it sets a standard before us that we can never keep. We are enslaved by our sin, which obstructs even our best efforts to keep the law. We are captive to both sin and the law, and we need a ransom.

> To live as a redeemed person is to live knowing that both the penalty and the power of sin have been broken.

In Mark's Gospel, we read, "Even the Son of Man came not to be served but to serve, and to give his life as a ransom for many" (10:45). And in 1 Peter, we learn what the ransom required: "You were ransomed from the futile ways inherited from your forefathers, not with perishable things such as silver or gold, but with the precious blood of Christ, like that of a lamb without blemish or spot" (1:18-19). The blood of Christ was shed to ransom you from the slavery of sin.

But do you live as a person who has been redeemed? Patty Hearst was a woman taken captive by the Symbionese Liberation Army in 1974 and held hostage for a time. But one of the most shocking parts of her story is that even after the ransom was given and she was free to go, she didn't leave. She stayed with her captors and joined them in a life of crime. What about you? Do you forget you've been set free and are no longer a slave to sin?

When faced with temptation, it can be all too easy to say, "I can't help it. I can't help that I gossip, covet, slander, hate…" But our Redeemer says, "Yes you can! I have bought you, ransomed you, and redeemed you, and you are no longer a slave to sin. You belong to me, and I have given you all you need for life and godliness." To live as a redeemed person is to live knowing that both the penalty *and the power* of sin have been broken. Sin no longer is your master because you have been redeemed.

If you are in Christ, you have been redeemed by the blood of the Lamb. Your ransom has been paid and you have been set free. Walk in the freedom he purchased for you.

JESUS THE PERFECT SACRIFICE

We marvel at stories of sacrifice: a soldier who throws himself on a grenade to save his platoon, or a woman who runs in front of a car to save a child about to be hit. Sacrifice, especially self-sacrifice, is astounding. Even Jesus told his disciples, "Greater love has no one than this, that someone lay down his life for his friends" (John 15:13). Then in the next verse, he said, "You are my friends." There is no greater love than that which Jesus has for us. He proves it by laying down his life.

In John's Gospel, among the first public proclamations is this from John the Baptist: "Behold, the Lamb of God, who takes away the sins of the world!" (1:29). This is one of those passages we might read with a numbing familiarity, so numbing that we barely blink an eye. But this scene in John's Gospel captures a seemingly strange man saying seemingly strange words, and this should cause us to stop and ask about what's being said. Why would John the Baptist point at Jesus and call him the Lamb of God? John was tying Jesus to two Old Testament concepts that his Jewish listeners would have been familiar with: the Passover lamb and the sacrificial lamb.

In chapter 5, we looked briefly at Exodus 12, which documents the tenth and final plague. The night before the Israelites were delivered out of captivity, God told them, through Moses, that he was about to send a plague that would bring about the death of all firstborn sons. However, God would make a provision that ensured the survival of their firstborns. Every Jewish family was to take a perfect lamb, slaughter it, and put the blood of the lamb on the doorframe of their home. That night, when the Lord saw the blood, he would pass over that house, and the firstborn son would live. This is the event that Passover observes, and in it, the pattern of redemption was set—the death and blood of a perfect lamb would save.

The night before Jesus's crucifixion, the Jewish Passover was observed. In Luke's Gospel, we read,

> When the hour came, he reclined at table, and the apostles with him. And he said to them, "I have earnestly desired to eat this Passover with you before I suffer. For I tell you I will not eat it until it is fulfilled in the kingdom of God." And he took a cup, and when he had given thanks he said, "Take this, and divide it among yourselves. For I tell you that from now on I will not drink of the fruit of the vine until the kingdom of God comes." And he took bread, and when he had given thanks, he broke it and gave it to them, saying, "This is my body, which is given for you. Do this in remembrance of me." And likewise the cup after they had

eaten, saying, "This cup that is poured out for you is
the new covenant in my blood" (22:14-20).

Jesus was showing his disciples that he was sent to be the Passover
lamb, the one without blemish who would be slaughtered so they
could live. His blood would save them.

But Jesus was also the sacrificial lamb. After the Israelites
crossed the Red Sea and met God at the base of Mount Sinai
(Exodus 1–18), God established his presence with them through
his law and his tabernacle (Exodus 19–40). Remember, the book
of Exodus ended with the glory of the Lord filling the tabernacle. As Dr. Jay Sklar says, "If you were an Israelite, all of this
[redemption, deliverance, the law, the tabernacle] would lead
to some burning questions: How in the world can the holy and
pure King of the universe dwell among his sinful and impure
people? How can he live here, in our very midst, without his
holiness melting us in our sin and impurity? Leviticus answers
these questions."[6]

I doubt that Leviticus is on anybody's short list of favorite
books in the Bible. It seems like a long and strange list of long
and strange rituals—ones that have very little to do with us today.
Truth be told, how often have you skipped over Leviticus in your
yearly Bible reading plan? Well, not anymore!

Leviticus reminds us that we, an unholy people, serve a holy
God. It reminds us that our sin is serious and the atonement of
sin requires sacrifice. Because sin is in us and around us constantly,
we have a proclivity to minimize its seriousness. And when we
minimize sin, we unavoidably minimize the atonement of that sin.
But sin is a big and horrible deal. It renders us unholy and unclean.
It permeates and defiles every fiber of our being. And it causes us
to be separated from God. Theologian Cornelius Plantinga said,

Christians have always measured sin, in part, by the suffering needed to atone for it. The ripping and writhing of a body on a cross, the bizarre metaphysical maneuver of using death to defeat death, the urgency of the summons to human beings to ally themselves with the events of Christ and with the person of these events, and then to make that person and those events the center of their lives—these things tell us that the main human trouble is desperately difficult to fix, even for God, and that sin is the longest-running of human emergencies.[7]

If we are to be redeemed, forgiven, and restored, our sin must be atoned for. And it took a sacrifice to atone for sin. But, the sacrifices prescribed in the Old Testament were given over and over and over—daily sacrifices, weekly sacrifices, monthly sacrifices, and yearly sacrifices—year after year after year. From the time of Leviticus onward, throughout the rest of the Old Testament, the question becomes, *Would it ever end?* Would sin ever be permanently and finally atoned for? Would there ever be a sacrifice pure enough to be a final offering?

The writer of Hebrews tells us:

Since the law has but a shadow of the good things to come instead of the true form of these realities, it can never, by the same sacrifices that are continually offered every year, make perfect those who draw near. Otherwise, would they not have ceased to be offered, since the worshipers, having once been cleansed, would no longer have any consciousness of sins? But in these sacrifices there is a reminder of sins every year. For it is impossible for the blood of bulls and goats to take away sins.

Consequently, when Christ came into the world, he said, "Sacrifices and offerings you have not desired, but a body have you prepared for me; in burnt offerings and sin offerings you have taken no pleasure. Then I said, 'Behold, I have come to do your will, O God, as it is written of me in the scroll of the book.'"

When he said above, "You have neither desired nor taken pleasure in sacrifices and offerings and burnt offerings and sin offerings" (these are offered according to the law), then he added, "Behold, I have come to do your will." He does away with the first in order to establish the second. And by that will we have been sanctified through the offering of the body of Jesus Christ once for all (10:1-10).

Did you catch the last three words? *Once for all.* One sacrifice, the body of Jesus, that atones for all time those who are being saved. There had never, in the history of the world, been a lamb pure enough, perfect enough to save once and for all—until the Lion of Judah took on flesh and willingly became the Lamb of God.

This wasn't an easy or cheap solution. It was costly beyond comprehension. But because the Lamb of God willingly placed himself on the altar, his sacrifice was acceptable and pleasing to the Father. And the glorious result is that you and I are cleansed from all our unrighteousness. Permanently. Completely. Finally.

One day, we will join the chorus of heaven and sing,

"Worthy is the Lamb who was slain, to receive power and wealth and wisdom and might and honor and glory and blessing!" And I heard every creature in heaven and on earth and under the earth and in the sea, and all that is in them, saying, "To him who sits on the throne and to the Lamb be blessing and honor and glory and might forever and ever!" And the four living creatures said, "Amen!" and the elders fell down and worshiped (Revelation 5:12-14).

Take some time today to worship the Lamb of God, who has taken away the sin of the world.

JESUS THE CONQUEROR

I've saved this picture until the end because it is the picture, I would argue, that our hearts might long for most—Jesus as our Champion, Victor, Conqueror. Oh, we like to convince ourselves we can fight our own battles and we can stand up for ourselves, but Scripture paints quite a different picture of both our enemy and us. We are more helpless and in greater danger than we ever imagine, and our enemy is stronger and more evil than we care to believe. We overestimate ourselves and underestimate our enemy. The truth is, we are in a battle we cannot win—and it is a battle for our very lives. We are cornered, trapped, and our defeat is sure.

> We have a conquering hero who stepped in and fought for us. He waged war on our behalf, and was victorious!

But praise be to God, we have a conquering hero who stepped in and fought for us. He waged war on our behalf, and was victorious!

Ever since God made the promise in Genesis 3:15 that he would send a seed of the woman to defeat the serpent, we have been waiting to see how this great victory would occur. Throughout the Old Testament, we are given glimpses of what it might look like, glimpses of what to expect. My favorite of these is found in 1 Samuel 17.

Most of us know the story of David and Goliath. We learned it as children and have most likely heard it taught as adults. It is the story of an unlikely champion and an unexpected victory. Sadly, most of us have probably been taught that the point of the story is to show us how we can be more like David—how we can fight the giants in our life if we just believe in God.

But David did not engage Goliath in a battle of life and death to show us how we, too, can fight giants—real or metaphorical. After all, nine-foot-tall bullies are not an everyday occurrence for most of us. But we do all face giant fears and struggles that loom large over us. However, if I'm honest, even these metaphorical giants are as undefeatable to me as Goliath was to the Israelites. Try as I might, I can't completely get rid of the sin in my life or the suffering that comes my way. And I certainly can't defeat my greatest enemy, death. We're more like the Israelites who were cowering in fear than like David, who marched courageously into battle. And, praise God, what was true for them is also true for us: The victory doesn't depend on us. We have a champion who did battle on our behalf.

We have one great enemy. Scripture calls him Satan, the devil, and the ancient serpent. And this enemy of our souls wields mighty weapons. He discourages us, lies to us, and reminds us of all the ways we fail. But the two greatest weapons this enemy wields are those of sin and death. Sin separates us from God, and death is the result of sin. Once sin entered the world, all were condemned to death because all have sinned.

However, our great champion, Jesus, came to wage war against our enemy and his weapons. As a result, sin and death have been utterly defeated! The child of God no longer lives under the penalty (death) or the power of sin. As Paul wrote in his letter to the Roman church:

> If we have been united with him in a death like his,
> we shall certainly be united with him in a resurrection
> like his. We know that our old self was crucified with
> him in order that the body of sin might be brought to
> nothing, so that we would no longer be enslaved to sin.
> For one who has died has been set free from sin. Now
> if we have died with Christ, we believe that we will
> also live with him. We know that Christ, being raised
> from the dead, will never die again; death no longer
> has dominion over him. For the death he died he died
> to sin, once for all, but the life he lives he lives to God.
> So you also must consider yourselves dead to sin and
> alive to God in Christ Jesus (Romans 6:5-11).

We have been set free from the enemy of sin, and we have been
delivered from the great and final enemy of death!

> Behold! I tell you a mystery. We shall not all sleep, but
> we shall all be changed, in a moment, in the twinkling
> of an eye, at the last trumpet. For the trumpet will
> sound, and the dead will be raised imperishable, and
> we shall be changed. For this perishable body must put
> on the imperishable, and this mortal body must put on
> immortality. When the perishable puts on the imper-
> ishable, and the mortal puts on immortality, then shall
> come to pass the saying that is written: "Death is swal-
> lowed up in victory." "O death, where is your victory?
> O death, where is your sting?" The sting of death is sin,
> and the power of sin is the law. But thanks be to God,
> who gives us the victory through our Lord Jesus Christ
> (1 Corinthians 15:51-57).

How did this victory occur? Jesus, the promised seed of the woman in Genesis 3, was sent to do battle on our behalf. He was sent to crush the head of the serpent. And he accomplished that victory on the cross. What's more is that when the enemy was defeated, his weapons also lost their power.

After David defeated Goliath, the men of Israel, who had been cowering in fear, ran after their champion, David. They followed the conquering hero onto the battlefield and received all the benefits of his victory.[8] They did not fight the battle. They did not earn the victory. And yet, they received the rewards of that victory because David had won the battle for them. In a similar but greater way, you and I don't fight the battle for our salvation; Jesus was sent to do that. But we do run after him, receiving all the benefits his victory has secured.

The five pictures of how Jesus saves—as the second Adam, Reconciler, Redeemer, Perfect Sacrifice, and Champion—each highlight a different aspect of his one salvation. Each helps us to better understand what Jesus was sent to do and what he accomplished on our behalf. Rest in the finished work of Christ and never cease to be amazed that Jesus is Immanuel—God with us.

Points to Remember from Chapter 7

- We are saved by works—not ours, but the perfect works of Christ.

- Jesus, as the second Adam, was sent to redo and, therefore, undo the effects of the first Adam's sins.

- Our Reconciler gives us peace with God.

- Our Redeemer ransoms us from slavery.

- Only one lamb was pure enough to remove all sin for all time—the spotless Lamb of God.

- Our Champion has come and won the battle on our behalf!

Discussion Questions

1. Which picture of the work of Christ means the most to you, and why?

   a. Second Adam

   b. Reconciler

   c. Redeemer

   d. Perfect Sacrifice

   e. Conqueror

2. How can you use one of these pictures to share the gospel with someone else?

3. How does it minister to your soul to be reminded, "This is not the way it is supposed to be"?

4. In the parable of the prodigal son (Luke 15:11-24), how does the father display the reconciliation God accomplishes in Christ?

5. Read Ephesians 2:11-22. Do you have a "dividing wall" between you and any other group of people? If so, how do these verses challenge you?

6. Read Ephesians 1:7. What observations and insights do you receive about redemption in this verse?

7. Read Romans 6:17-18. Describe two or three ways you could be a slave to righteousness.

8. Read Exodus 14:13-14. Who would do the fighting? What would the people see? What would happen to their enemy? How does this showcase God's ultimate salvation?

9. Either write below or share with your group one point, truth, or lesson that either challenged or encouraged you from this chapter.

For Further Study

If you are still in Adam, all that was true of Adam is true of you. If you are in Christ, then Jesus has given his status to you—not because you earned or accomplished that status, but because Jesus gives the victory that was his to all who believe in him. Using the chart below, make a brief comment in the last column about what that means for you now.

	Adam	Jesus	Me
Obedience	Disobedient	Obedient	
	Genesis 3:6	Romans 5:19	Galatians 2:20
Temptation	Tempted and Satan won	Tempted and Jesus won	
	Genesis 3:1-7	Luke 4:1-13	Hebrews 2:18
Curse	Brought the curse	Bears and breaks the curse	
	Genesis 3:14-19	Galatians 3:13	Galatians 3:13
Death/Life	Brings death	Brings life	
	Genesis 5 1 Corinthians 15:21	Romans 5:17-18 1 Corinthians 15:21	1 Corinthians 15:22
Paradise	Out of paradise	Into paradise	
	Genesis 3:23-24	John 14:3; Revelation 22:2	Luke 23:43

CHAPTER 8

THE 50 MOST IMPORTANT DAYS IN THE HISTORY OF THE WORLD

Scripture Memory

"There is salvation in no one else, for there is no other name under heaven given among men by which we must be saved" (Acts 4:12).

Pray

"I do not cease to give thanks for you, remembering you in my prayers, that the God of our Lord Jesus Christ, the Father of glory, may give you the Spirit of wisdom and of revelation in the knowledge of him, having the eyes of your hearts enlightened, that you may know what is the hope to which he has called you, what are the riches of his glorious inheritance in the saints, and what is the immeasurable greatness of his power toward us who believe, according to the working of his great might that he worked in Christ when he raised him from the dead and seated him at his right hand in the heavenly places" (Ephesians 1:16-20). Father, I join Paul in praying for the Spirit of wisdom and the opening of my spiritual eyes. Thank you for the hope that is mine because Jesus is seated on his heavenly throne.

In the introduction, I mentioned that most of us have probably spent our Christian life explaining our faith and salvation to others by telling them, "Jesus died on the cross to forgive me of my sins, and to take me to live with him forever in heaven." While this is true, the statement is far too brief a synopsis, too truncated a version of the story of our redemption. We have spent time looking at the scope of our redemption as well as the depths, heights, lengths, and breadths the Lord has gone to accomplish that redemption: He is washing us, restoring us, and making us into his own children because he longs to be with us again. In chapter 1, we also spent time looking at the importance of the historical reality of the story. It is of utmost importance that these events happened in real

> The cross is the center point of our salvation. It is the defining moment, the place where the great battle for our souls was fought—and won.

time, in real places, with real people. I will say it again: We are saved because a real man was really born, really died, and really rose again.

Several years ago, a young woman in my Bible study gave a brief testimony of how and when the Lord saved her. She told us about her childhood and high school years in fairly broad terms, but then, in great detail, she told us about the events of a particular Wednesday night during her college years. She told us about what happened that night and about her conversation the next morning in a specific location—a friend's dorm room. She told us how the Lord used the events of that 24-hour period to bring her to salvation.

Just as there are some days and experiences that stand out as crucial moments in time for our individual stories, the same is true of the big story of redemption. With that in mind, we are going to look now at the 50 most important days in the history of the world—from the cross to Pentecost.

CRUCIFIXION

The cross. We sing about it, talk about it, and even decorate with it. The cross is a symbol of our faith. But, at times, we are in danger of becoming so accustomed to having a cross dangle from our ears, hang around our necks, and decorate our walls that we forget it represents torture, brutality, and death. As Robert Peterson notes:

> Christians chose Christ's cross as their emblem. On the one hand, this is amazing because the cross spoke of crucifixion, which was regarded with horror in the ancient world...On the other hand, in light of Paul's sentiment, "But far be it from me to boast except in the cross of our Lord Jesus Christ" (Gal. 6:14), they chose well. Why? Because the cross describes where the work of salvation was accomplished.[1]

Even though I have said several times that our salvation is more than the summary statement "Jesus died on the cross to save me from my sins," it is never less than that. The cross is the center point of our salvation. It is the defining moment, the place where the great battle for our souls was fought—and won. The cross is what Jesus was born for, where he was headed, and the location of the greatest battle ever fought.

Jesus told his disciples that he "came...to give his life as a ransom for many" (Mark 10:45). Jesus was a man on a mission. He knew what he had been sent to do. He knew he had been born to die. But knowing this and doing it are two different things. Lest we ever forget, in no way did Jesus's knowledge or determination make his sacrifice easier. Three times on the night before his crucifixion, Jesus, in the Garden of Gethsemane, asked his Father, "If it be possible, let this cup pass from me; nevertheless, not as I will, but as you will" (Matthew 26:39).

But there's a big difference between what happened in the first garden and the second. Remember, he was sent to undo what happened in the first garden. Jesus, in a garden, knowing he had been sent to fulfill the promise made in the first garden, knowing he had been sent to reclaim all that was lost in the first garden, asked his Father, "Is there any other way?" And the Father answered, "No." Why? Because Jesus is the way, the only way—he is the way, the truth, and the life, and no one comes to the Father except through him (John 14:6). And so he did what Adam should have done: he obeyed.

Jesus knew the cross was his to endure. He knew that it was the Father's will and the Father's way. And so he went, willingly and obediently, in our place.

The death of Jesus was foretold in Isaiah 53:4-7:

> Surely he has borne our griefs and carried our sorrows; yet we esteemed him stricken, smitten by God, and afflicted. But he was pierced for our transgressions; he was crushed for our iniquities; upon him was the chastisement that brought us peace, and with his wounds we are healed. All we like sheep have gone astray; we have turned—every one—to his own way; and the LORD has laid on him the iniquity of us all. He was oppressed, and he was afflicted, yet he opened not his mouth; like a lamb that is led to the slaughter, and like a sheep that before its shearers is silent, so he opened not his mouth.

Look at the pronouns. One singular person (he, him, his) would experience the unimaginable on behalf of many (our, we, us). He would bear and carry our griefs and sorrows. He would be pierced, crushed, oppressed, and afflicted. He would have our iniquity laid on him. And, as a result, we would have peace, be healed, and, according to verse 11, be "accounted righteous." As Paul wrote in Romans, "As by the one man's disobedience the many were made sinners, so by the one man's obedience the many will be made righteous" (5:19).

Peterson says,

> The innocent Servant suffers willingly. "He poured out his soul to death" (v. 12). He does so as a Sin-Bearer in the place of others; he takes the punishment that they deserve. The Servant's substitutionary death has amazing results. His death accomplished justification; it makes "many to be accounted righteous" (v. 11). His death is an "offering for guilt" (v. 10), which according to Leviticus makes "atonement" and procures forgiveness (Lev. 5:16, 18).[2]

And Jesus did it all willingly! He could have saved himself (Mark 15:30), but he didn't. Astoundingly, the author of Hebrews tells us why: "Jesus...for the joy that was set before him endured the cross, despising the shame, and is seated at the right hand of the throne of God" (Hebrews 12:2).

This all happened at the cross. The cross of Christ, the place of so much suffering, is also the place of so much victory. It's the paradox of the gospel—life comes through death. The cross, that which was intended to shame and kill, became that which removes shame and gives life. This is why the cross is the symbol of our faith. In 1912, George Bennard wrote the following lyrics about that cross:

On a hill far away stood an old rugged cross,
the emblem of suffering and shame;
and I love that old cross where the dearest and best
for a world of lost sinners was slain.

So I'll cherish the old rugged cross,
till my trophies at last I lay down;
I will cling to the old rugged cross,
and exchange it some day for a crown.[3]

The cross of Christ is our only hope.

RESURRECTION

I love Easter morning! In my family, Easter was the holiday with the most established family traditions. When the children were young, I would wake each one up by whispering in his or her ear, "He is risen." And each child would sleepily respond, "He is risen, indeed!" Even now, with my adult, married children living in other states, I text them "He is risen" every Easter morning. They love me enough to indulge me, and they text back, "He is risen, indeed!"

When all the children were still at home and we lived on our 15 acres in Kansas, I would wake everyone up before sunrise. They would, one by one, stumble into the kitchen, grab a cup of coffee or hot chocolate and a big blanket, and we would make our way out to a little dock that sat on our pond. We would sit side by side in a row with our feet dangling off the edge, and face eastward. As we sat there, we took turns choosing praise songs to sing. I've never sung an on-key note in my entire life, but the singing was beautiful and glorious, nonetheless. Together, as the sun rose, we worshipped the Son who had risen.

The death and resurrection of Jesus could be called the hinge of our entire salvation. And it is important to note that both his death and resurrection were essential. If Jesus had merely been a good man who happened to have died a horrible death, how would that have helped us? Throughout history, there have been many good men who have died terrible deaths. But Jesus was not just a good man, he was a perfect man. He was fully man and fully God. And his death was on our behalf. He took the punishment we deserved and died in our place. And, as we will see, his death was swallowed up in victory when he rose triumphantly over the grave.

But think about this: Up until the morning of the resurrection, no one knew yet that anything unusual, special, new, or different had happened. Looking back, knowing what we know now, we marvel at the miracle of the manger, Jesus's sinless life, and his death on the cross. But, if you and I had been alive during that time, I'm not sure we would have recognized how unique Jesus was. Other babies had been born, and other men had been crucified. But once the resurrection took place, everything changed.

Our entire faith rests on the resurrection. Paul said,

> If there is no resurrection of the dead, then not even Christ has been raised. And if Christ has not been raised, then our preaching is in vain and your faith is in vain. We are even found to be misrepresenting God, because we testified about God that he raised Christ, whom he did not raise if it is true that the dead are not raised. For if the dead are not raised, not even Christ has been raised. And if Christ has not been raised, your faith is futile and you are still in your sins. Then those also who have fallen asleep in Christ have perished. If in Christ we have hope in this life only, we are of all people most to be pitied (1 Corinthians 15:13-19).

But our hope is not in vain! Thanks be to God that

> in fact Christ has been raised from the dead, the first-fruits of those who have fallen asleep. For as by a man came death, by a man has come also the resurrection of the dead. For as in Adam all die, so also in Christ shall all be made alive (verses 20-22).

Jesus is the second Adam and, as such, he undoes the effects of the first Adam. In chapters 2 and 3 of this book, we read about how the goodness of God's creation was affected by the great disruption that came because of our first parents' sin. In Genesis 2:17, God told them what would happen if they rebelled against him: "Of the tree of the knowledge of good and evil you shall not eat, for in the day that you eat of it you shall surely die." Death was ushered in the moment

> Our hope, as those who are in Christ, is that because Jesus's human body was raised from the dead, our human bodies will be raised from the dead as well.

Eve swallowed the fruit. But Jesus, the one promised in Genesis 3:15, was sent to swallow up the devastation and consequences of that rebellion. Death was swallowed up by death:

> Behold! I tell you a mystery. We shall not all sleep, but we shall all be changed, in a moment, in the twinkling of an eye, at the last trumpet. For the trumpet will sound, and the dead will be raised imperishable, and we shall be changed. For this perishable body must put on the imperishable, and this mortal body must put on immortality. When the perishable puts on the

> imperishable, and the mortal puts on immortality,
> then shall come to pass the saying that is written:
> "Death is swallowed up in victory." "O death, where
> is your victory? O death, where is your sting?"
> (1 Corinthians 15:51-55).

We will be raised because he has been raised! The hope of the resurrection is tied tightly to the humanity of Christ. We have talked about how Jesus was fully God and fully man—and the full humanity of Christ is so important in the hope of our resurrection. The man Jesus was a human being who experienced hunger, thirst, fear, exhaustion, and then death. His deity did not prevent him from experiencing his humanity. And it was his human body that was killed and raised. Our hope, as those who are in Christ, is that because Jesus's human body was raised from the dead, our human bodies will be raised from the dead as well.

Christianity is the only religion in the world that claims and celebrates an empty tomb. Muhammad is in his grave. Buddha is in his grave. There is only one empty tomb: that of our risen Lord Jesus. He is risen. He is risen, indeed!

ASCENSION

The title for this chapter is "The 50 Most Important Days in the History of the World." We are looking at the events that occurred on Good Friday, Easter Sunday, skipping over the 40 days when the resurrected Jesus walked on earth in his resurrected body, then picking up again with the day he ascended into heaven, and ending with Pentecost.

I keep mentioning that we can't start with the story at its midpoint. If we do, we will miss so much. But, in the same way that people are inclined to start the story of salvation at the cross, they are inclined to end with the resurrection. But there is more! We looked at the fact it is not enough for Rapunzel to merely be out of the tower; we want to see her returned to the kingdom and restored to her parents. We long for full restoration.

The ascension of Christ is key in our understanding of where the Bible's story is headed—full restoration. As we look at each of the key events that occurred during those 50 days, we see that the good news for us keeps getting better and better! At the cross, our sins are forgiven. At the empty tomb, we receive victory over death. And at the ascension, we see that this story keeps heading up—literally.

In Acts 1, we read that while Jesus was standing and talking with the disciples, he was "lifted up, and a cloud took him out of their sight" (verse 9). As the disciples stood there, "gazing into heaven as he went, behold, two men stood by them in white robes, 'Men of Galilee, why do you stand looking into heaven? This Jesus, who was taken up from you into heaven, will come in the same way as you saw him go into heaven'" (verses 10-11). In John's Gospel, Jesus told his disciples that "no one has ascended into heaven except he who descended from heaven, the Son of Man" (3:13). This means the ascension is tied to the incarnation. It is not an isolated event, but a continuation of what Jesus was sent to do.

I can't help but think of the great rescue of Jessica McClure. I was in college in Oklahoma in October 1987 when 18-month-old Jessica fell into a well in Midland, Texas. All of America watched with bated breath for three days to see if this little girl, wounded yet alive, could be rescued from the bottom of a narrow and collapsing well casing. The entire mission, from start to finish, defied all odds. Jessica was too far down. The casing was too narrow. And yet, rescued she was!

It took the rescue workers the vast majority of those three days just to reach Jessica. There was great rejoicing when they reached her, but the victory was far from complete, for reaching her was not enough. The descent to Jessica was not the ultimate goal. They had to bring her up safely. The descent was vital, but the rescue journey wasn't complete until Jessica had ascended to the top of the well.

Jesus was sent on a much greater rescue mission, and it, too, started with a great descent. God the Son set aside his crown and robe, put on human flesh, confined himself to the womb of a woman, and condescended to letting his fleshly feet be covered with the very dirt he had created. He went even further when he wrapped a towel around his waist and washed similar dirt off his disciples' feet. But the road kept going further down still. The descent didn't end until he was nailed to a cross, suffered unimaginable pain, breathed his last, and cried out, "It is finished" (John 19:30). He descended to the depths because that is where you and I lay—not wounded, but dead. And it took a descent to death to rescue us from death.

But the road didn't end at the cross! It turned and headed back up. The stone was rolled away, and Jesus walked out of the tomb—death could not hold him. He is not just the crucified Savior; he is the risen Savior. And he is not just the risen Savior, he is the ascended Lord. At the ascension, we see Jesus continuing back up, all the way to full restoration.

The ascension of Christ was the "linchpin of Christ's saving work bridging his earthly and heavenly ministries."[4] It was the victorious re-entry of the conquering King. He won the battle and returned to the throne room as the rightful King—and he made it possible for his bride, the church, to go with him. It was also the acceptable entry of the great, perfect, and final High Priest into the Holy of Holies. This is why we can "with confidence draw near to the throne of grace, that we may receive mercy and find grace to help in time of need" (Hebrews 4:16). Jesus is there, and has secured our access.

SESSION

When a king is on his throne, it is said that his court is in session. When Congress is assembled, we say they are in session. To be in session means that a ruler (or ruling body) is in place to work for the good of those he (or the body) governs.

At the time of Jesus's ascension, more than 400 years had passed since the last king of Israel was on his throne, and nearly 1,000 years since David was on his. Yet the Jewish people had been longing for a Davidic king. Why? Because they knew the promises God had given in 2 Samuel 7. And they knew that whatever their covenant-making God had promised, he would fulfill.

Not only had God promised David an eternal throne and kingdom through the prophet Isaiah, he said this promised one would rule and reign over all things:

> To us a child is born, to us a son is given; and the government shall be upon his shoulder, and his name shall be called Wonderful Counselor, Mighty God, Everlasting Father, Prince of Peace. Of the increase of his government and of peace there will be no end, on the throne of David and over his kingdom, to establish it and to uphold it with justice and with righteousness from this time forth and forevermore. The zeal of the LORD of hosts will do this (Isaiah 9:6-7).

When the angel came to Mary to tell her she was going to carry the Son of God, he said,

> Do not be afraid, Mary, for you have found favor with God. And behold, you will conceive in your womb

and bear a son, and you shall call his name Jesus. He will be great and will be called the Son of the Most High. And the Lord God will give to him the throne of his father David, and he will reign over the house of Jacob forever, and of his kingdom there will be no end (Luke 1:30-33).

Heaven itself declared that Jesus was the long-awaited King of all kings. He was the one who would be seated on the eternal throne, carry the government upon his shoulders, and establish his kingdom and his throne forever.

But Jesus didn't appear to be much of a king in the beginning. He was born in a stable to a carpenter and a peasant girl. He wandered the dusty roads of Galilee with "nowhere to lay his head" (Matthew 8:20). Instead of a mighty army, he had a ragtag group of 12 common men following him. Instead of overthrowing Israel's Roman oppressors, he merely irritated them. And at the end of his life, he was crucified as a common criminal. How could this possibly be the one the people were waiting for? If the story ended at the cross, it would be hard to see how Jesus was the long-awaited King.

We've seen that the road to the cross was the great descent, and from there, the road turned and began the ascent. The road didn't end until Jesus was again seated at the right hand of the Father (Hebrews 10:12). In Ephesians 1:20-22, we read that not only was Jesus seated at the right hand of God, but all things have been put "under his feet."

How do we know all this? We have eyewitnesses to almost every other aspect of Jesus's saving work. People saw his birth. They saw his crucifixion, resurrection, and even his ascension. We have eyewitness accounts of the mighty acts of God. But how do we know Jesus is seated on his eternal throne?

Well, we have eyewitnesses to that too. When Stephen was being stoned to death, he "gazed into heaven and saw the glory of God, and Jesus standing at the right hand of God. And he said, 'Behold, I see the heavens opened, and the Son of Man standing at the right hand of God'" (Acts 7:55-56). And in Revelation, John wrote that he "the one who conquers, I will grant him to sit with me on my throne" (Revelation 3:21). God has given us eyewitness accounts of the ascended Jesus on his throne.

We can be sure that Jesus is seated on his throne right now. And what is he doing? He is reigning and ruling over all things, including the circumstances of your life. Scripture tells us that Jesus, who is also our great high priest and can "sympathize with our weaknesses" (Hebrews 4:15), is currently interceding for us from the throne (Romans 8:34). Meaning, Jesus is on his throne, reigning, ruling, and praying for you right now.

We have a good, righteous, powerful, and loving King who rules and reigns for our good. And his court is in session.

PENTECOST

This great story of redemption has, from the beginning, been a work of our triune God: planned by the Father, accomplished by the Son, and applied by the Holy Spirit. The Father, Son, and Holy Spirit have been working together all through the story, starting from the very first page of Scripture. Throughout the Old Testament, it was primarily the Father who was in the spotlight. In the incarnation—with Jesus coming to earth—the Son came to the front of the stage. However, after the ascension, the Spirit steps into the spotlight.

In John 16:7, the day before the crucifixion, Jesus said to his frightened disciples, "I tell you the truth: it is to your advantage that I go away, for if I do not go away, the Helper will not come to you. But if I go, I will send him to you." Can you imagine being one of the disciples and hearing Jesus say it would be better for you if he went away? Jesus was the one they had left jobs and families for, the one they had placed all their hopes on. And now, not only was he telling them he was leaving, but that his departure would be best for them! Let's look at why and how that was true.

Back in chapter 6, what did we learn the Israelites in exile needed most? A new heart. In Ezekiel 36, God promised a day was coming when he would bring about that change.

And Pentecost was the fulfillment of that promise! As Sinclair Ferguson writes, "Pentecost publicly marks the transition from the old to the new covenant and signifies the commencement of the 'now' of the day of salvation (2 Cor 6:2)."[5] It was at Pentecost that the kingdom of God was fully inaugurated.

This is what happened:

> When the day of Pentecost arrived, they were all together in one place. And suddenly there came from heaven a sound like a mighty rushing wind, and it filled the entire house where they were sitting. And divided tongues as of fire appeared to them and rested on each one of them. And they were all filled with the Holy Spirit and began to speak in other tongues as the Spirit gave them utterance (Acts 2:1-4).

As I have said, the story keeps getting better and better. The road of exaltation keeps going higher and higher. But what could be better than Jesus seated on his heavenly throne? How about God himself coming down to dwell in the hearts of his people?

The Father sent the Son, and the Father and the Son sent the Spirit. God himself now dwells in the hearts of his children through the pouring out of his Holy Spirit. Christ dwells in us because he has poured his Spirit into our hearts. And God in us is even better than God next to us, which is why it was better for Jesus to go away. The new covenant, promised in Ezekiel 36 and fulfilled at Pentecost, accomplished that which the old covenants could not—holiness of life, made possible because the Holy Spirit now dwells in the hearts of God's people.

And it's not just individual believers who have the Holy Spirit dwelling in them, the Spirit also dwells in the corporate people of God. The tabernacle, and later, the temple, were the places where the presence of God was to be mediated to the rest of the world. The first temple was destroyed in 587 BC, and the second temple was destroyed in AD 70. But Jesus says that he himself is building a new temple. Ephesians 2 tells us,

> You are no longer strangers and aliens, but you are fellow citizens with the saints and members of the household of God, built on the foundation of the apostles and prophets, Christ Jesus himself being the cornerstone, in whom the whole structure, being joined together, grows into a holy temple in the Lord. In him you also are being built together into a dwelling place for God by the Spirit (verses 19-22).

And that which the Spirit builds, the Spirit fills.

The dwelling of God is not merely *with* his people, but *in* his people. And amazingly, this isn't the end of the story. There is still more good news to come!

Points to Remember from Chapter 8

- The cross reminds us that there is no other way to the Father.

- The ultimate battle of all time was fought—and won—on the cross.

- The resurrection of Jesus is what guarantees our resurrection.

- The ascension is the victorious re-entry of the conquering King, back into the presence of his Father.

- Jesus is seated on his throne, and his court is in session.

- God fills his new temple, the people of God, with his presence through the indwelling of the Holy Spirit.

- The incarnate, crucified, risen, and ascended Jesus has returned to the throne room and sat down at the right hand of the Father. His saving work is truly finished.

Discussion Questions

1. Read John 14:6. What is the way to the Father? Who comes to the Father through another way?

2. Read Mark 15:30. What could Jesus have done? What do you think kept him there (read Hebrews 12:2)?

3. Read 1 Corinthians 15:50-58. What is completely "swallowed up"? How does/should that change the way you live today? Why?

4. Read the glorious words of Revelation 1:17-18. Who is speaking? What is his command to John (verse 17)? On what is the command based (verse 18)? In what ways does the same truth ask you to "fear not" today?

5. Given the circumstances of your life today, why do you find hope in knowing that Jesus is seated on his throne and all things are under his feet?

6. Read Hebrews 6:19-20. What has the ascension won for you?

7. Read Romans 8:31-35. What are some ways you are helped by the truth that no one can condemn you because the king is on his throne and he himself—the one seated at the right hand of God—is interceding for you?

8. In what ways do we, as the new temple, serve some of the same purposes as the first temple?

9. Either write below or share with your group one point, truth, or lesson that either challenged or encouraged you from this chapter.

For Further Study

1. Read Ephesians 2:4-6. List the three things God has done. How do those line up with what Christ has done? Read verse 7. Where do we have to be to receive these things?

2. Compare Ephesians 1:20 with Ephesians 2:5-6. From what was Jesus raised? From what are we raised? Where is Christ seated? Where are we seated?

Ephesians 1:20	Ephesians 2:5-6
He worked in Christ when he raised him from the dead and seated him at his right hand in the heavenly places.	Even when we were dead in our trespasses, [he] made us alive together with Christ—by grace you have been saved—and raised us up with him and seated us with him in the heavenly places in Christ Jesus.

3. Read the following verses and write down what they
tell us about the work of the Spirit in us.

   • John 15:26-27

   • John 16:7-11

   • John 16:12-15

   • Romans 8:5-11

   • 2 Thessalonians 2:13

   • Galatians 5:22-23

CHAPTER 9

WAITING FOR OUR KING TO RETURN

Scripture Memory

"Jesus came and said to them, 'All authority in heaven and on earth has been given to me. Go therefore and make disciples of all nations, baptizing them in the name of the Father and of the Son and of the Holy Spirit, teaching them to observe all that I have commanded you. And behold, I am with you always, to the end of the age'" (Matthew 28:18-20).

Pray

> *"Whatever you do, in word or deed, do everything in the*
> *name of the Lord Jesus, giving thanks to God the Father*
> *through him" (Colossians 3:17). Father, may what I say*
> *and what I do be consistent with the story I am in.*

I have stressed that the Bible was never intended to merely be a list of doctrines we are to intellectually conquer or a series of standalone truth statements to be individually applied to our lives. Rather, it is the story of God working in our world on our behalf. We have spent the last eight chapters looking how God has been doing that, and making all things right again, calling a people to himself so he can be their God and dwell with them.

We've been following the storyline as it progressed from "once upon a time" to "but then an evil serpent," all the way to our great hero, who came and defeated our evil enemy. We have not done this merely for the purpose of being informed; we have done this so that we will be transformed. In the introduction, I warned that you were not, for one minute, going to be able to just sit back and enjoy the show. This drama of redemption, this grand story of how God works in our world for our salvation, is intended to invite you in, call you onto the stage, and transform you into an active participant. The story of each of our lives fits within God's bigger story—we are to live our daily trials, victories, joys, sorrows, fears, and celebrations in the context of the bigger story. We don't want to lose sight of the fact we were created to be participants in this bigger story, not observers living outside of it.

We ended the previous chapter with the glorious outpouring of the Holy Spirit. From the day of Pentecost until now, all believers have been unalterably "sealed for the day of redemption" (Ephesians 4:30) by God himself, who dwells in his people. But the indwelling of the Holy Spirit is just a foretaste of what is to come. God has promised that he will return for his people and will dwell with us for all eternity. That is our glorious hope of what is to come.

> The story of each of our lives fits within God's bigger story—we are to live our daily trials, victories, joys, sorrows, fears, and celebrations in the context of the bigger story.

But what about now? Where does that leave us? We are in between the first and second comings of Christ; we find ourselves living in the time between the great rescue and the great conclusion. So what do we do as we wait? Sit and twiddle our thumbs? Entertain ourselves? Try to be good people who go to church on Sunday and maybe a weekly Bible study or two thrown in for good measure? Tell a couple of people about Jesus?

Some believers wonder how we are to go about making a connection between what we read in the Bible and how we live it out. One of the more important questions we can ask ourselves is, How does my faith affect the moments, days, weeks, and years of my life? Or more simply, How do I live out my faith? If the Bible is the great drama that we have been saying it is, where is the script for our part in the play? The intent of this chapter is to help us answer that question.

In his book *The Drama of Doctrine*, Kevin Vanhoozer wrote that all of history could be divided as if it were a five-act play: Act 1 is the story of creation and the fall. Like the introduction to any good story, we are introduced to the characters, themes, setting, and conflict. We know who the drama will be about, where it will take place, and what problem will need to be solved. Act 2 is the story of God creating and establishing Israel. We can see the rising action in the drama of redemption. As good readers, we are meant to ask, When will the great conflict be resolved? When and how will the characters be saved? Act 3 is the birth and life of Jesus—the great high point in the narrative! In Act 3, we see how the great conflict is resolved and how the characters are rescued. Act 4 begins with Pentecost and goes through to the end of the age. But we have only the first scene of Act 4 before the drama jumps to the last act, Act 5. This is the final consummation of all things in the new heavens and the new earth.[1] We see how the story will end.

So, we have the script for the first three acts as well as the final act. We know how the story begins, progresses, and ends.

And this is where our stories fit in! We are living in Act 4, between the birth of the church and the final act. Vanhoozer asks,

"'Now' is our scene. How shall we play it?"[2] Alasdair MacIntyre answers this way: "I can only answer the question 'what am I to do?' …if I can answer the prior question, 'Of what story or stories do I find myself a part?'"[3] We know the story we are in, so how do we live our lives in light of it?

If you were in New York City at the Minskoff Theatre on Broadway watching *The Lion King*, and suddenly the person playing Simba began quoting the monologue from *Hamlet*, "To be, or not to be, that is the question," you would wonder what was going on. Why? Because you would know his words and actions didn't fit. They aren't part of the storyline, and they aren't in the script. If the actor were to later explain that he was simply improvising, you would know that he wasn't doing a good job of it. He wasn't following the trajectory of the story. His words and actions were not helping the story move from where it started to where it would end.

That is the point Williams and Vanhoozer are making. We might not have a script for our lives, but here's what we do know: We know what story we are in, how the story began, and how the story will end. Therefore, we can live in a way that both embodies and furthers the storyline, and is consistent with the "script."

We are in a story that stretches from before time began and reaches into eternity; we are in the story of how the Maker of heaven and earth is redeeming his good creation and restoring it to all it was intended to be. We are in the great drama of the redemption of all things, and we have a part to play.

IMAGE BEARING

> God created man in his own image, in the image of God
> he created him; male and female he created them. And
> God blessed them. And God said to them, "Be fruitful

and multiply and fill the earth and subdue it, and have dominion over the fish of the sea and over the birds of the heavens and over every living thing that moves on the earth" (Genesis 1:27-28).

God "is the same yesterday and today and forever" (Hebrews 13:8). His purposes and plans stand firm forever (Psalm 33:11). His mission has never changed. If we are going to live in a way that faithfully embodies the storyline, we need to recognize that the goal of the mission God gave to his people has not changed. This mission—entrusted to Adam, Eve, Noah, Abraham, Moses, Israel, David, and, ultimately, Jesus—is now given to us to carry out. As you look through the Scriptures, ask yourself, *Am I doing this? Am I participating in the drama of redemption in a way that is consistent with the storyline and faithfully embodies the script?* Because the scene you and I have been called to play is now!

In chapter 2, we looked at the mandate given to Adam and Eve in the garden: "Be fruitful and multiply and fill the earth and subdue it, and have dominion over the fish of the sea and over the birds of the heavens and over every living thing that moves on the earth" (Genesis 1:28). What was the scope of their mission? They were to fill the whole earth. What were they to do? They were to be fruitful, multiply, have dominion, and fill the earth with the glory of God. Who were they to be? Image bearers. Has God changed his mind or his mission? No!

Adam and Eve were created in God's image. When they rebelled, the ability to accurately reflect his image was lost. We now have to be conformed and transformed back into his image. In Romans 8:29, Paul wrote that "those whom he foreknew he also predestined to be conformed to the image of his Son." Part of the work God will do in us in this life is make us look more like Jesus.

Now, this transformation requires our participation! We have to renew our minds (Romans 12:1-2) and participate with God's work in us to transform us. We have to put off the old self and put on the new—the one that more accurately bears the image of God (Ephesians 4:22, 24). We call this sanctification, which simply refers to the slow process of becoming more like Jesus. It includes dying to sin and walking in righteousness. This process happens as we study God's Word and obey it; as we confess, repent, and believe; and as we pursue the high calling to be holy as God is holy.

We are image bearers in all we do—as we cook, create, study, strategize, pray, play, think, teach, worship, work—in every area of life. However, we bear this image in a way that is marred by sin, so our image bearing is imperfect. That is why we must be re-created in the image of God.

As we are conformed more and more to the image of Christ, we are being restored into all that God created us to be, which means that we are more and more able to reflect his image in all areas of our lives. And that is the truest sense of human flourishing—to be all that God created us to be.

BE FRUITFUL AND MULTIPLY

You may have heard it said that we all have a dash—that line on our tombstone that is between the year we were born and the year we die. Mine will be "1967–?" The question for every one of us is, *What are you doing with your dash?* Understanding our role in the story is the only way we will ever live our dash in the way we were created to live it.

Who are we? Image bearers. What are we to do? Be fruitful and fill the earth with God's glory. But what does it mean for us to "be fruitful and multiply"? In Genesis 1:28 it meant exactly what it sounds like it means—to have babies. This was how Adam and

Eve were going to fill the earth. They were to have children, raise them to know and obey the word of the Lord, and fill the earth with people who knew and worshipped the living God.

> As we are conformed more and more to the image of Christ, we are being restored into all that God created us to be.

What about those of us in today's church? Participating in the mission of God *can* include having children, but there are also other significant ways we can help to fill the earth with people who know, love, and worship the living God.

In Colossians 1:3-10, we read,

> We always thank God, the Father of our Lord Jesus Christ, when we pray for you, since we heard of your faith in Christ Jesus and of the love that you have for all the saints, because of the hope laid up for you in heaven. Of this you have heard before in the word of the truth, the gospel, which has come to you, as indeed in the whole world it is *bearing fruit and increasing*—as it also does among you, since the day you heard it and understood the grace of God in truth...And so, from the day we heard, we have not ceased to pray for you, asking that you may be filled with the knowledge of his will in all spiritual wisdom and understanding, so as to walk in a manner worthy of the Lord, fully pleasing to him: *bearing fruit* in every good work and *increasing* in the knowledge of God (emphasis added).

Did you notice what is bearing fruit and increasing? It is the gospel! Gregory Beale helpfully explains:

> The implication is that the notion of physical newborn children "increasing and multiplying" in the original Genesis 1:28 commission now includes people who have left their old way of life, have become spiritually newborn, and have come to reflect the image of God's glorious presence...[and we can] view the literal commission about progeny to be interpreted in the new age as the increase of the reception of God's word in new believers and the multiplication of believers.[4]

In other words, the gospel itself bears fruit and multiplies image bearers. So one way we are to now be fruitful and multiply is by allowing the gospel to increase in us and by sharing it, and making disciples out of other image bearers as we do.

The memory passage for this chapter is Matthew 28:18-20. These were some of Jesus's last words to his disciples. We call this statement the Great Commission—the marching orders given by the King to his subjects. This is what we are to do while we wait for him to return—we are to fill the earth with people who know, love, and worship Jesus. This is what our side of covenantal faithfulness looks like.

As we trace the threads of the story, we look to see how Jesus is the ultimate fulfillment of each part. He is the faultless Adam: the perfect image of God, the one who has all dominion. He is the final Abraham: the one sent from his home to the place God told him to go and the ultimate blessing to all the families of the earth. He is the perfect Israelite: He is truly holy as his Father is holy. The problem is that we stop there. Are all of God's promises fulfilled in Jesus? Yes! But fulfillment does not mean the story has ended. We don't close the book after the resurrection because the story is not over yet. We need to know how the story is to be carried on by us. Fulfilled in Jesus? Yes, but still to be carried out by us.

DOMINION AND RIGHTEOUS RULE

> God created man in his own image, in the image of God
> he created him; male and female he created them. And
> God blessed them. And God said to them, "Be fruitful
> and multiply and *fill the earth and subdue it, and have
> dominion* over the fish of the sea and over the birds of
> the heavens and over every living thing that moves on
> the earth" (Genesis 1:27-28, emphasis added).

If you have seen Disney's *The Lion King*, you know what the
opening scene looks like as the sun rises over the Serengeti. The
land is beautiful, the animals are flourishing, and the world is
functioning as it should. Why? Because the good king Mufasa is
on his throne. But what happens to the land when Mufasa's evil
brother, Scar, becomes king? It dries up and the animals starve.
Why? Because when dominion is used for evil, everything suffers.
God gives dominion so his creation will flourish.

In Matthew 28, we read that Jesus has all authority in heaven
and on earth. As a result of this authority, he tells us to go into all
the earth and make disciples. Like Adam and Eve, we have been
given dominion. I had a professor ask me one time, "Who is flourishing because of your influence?" I now ask myself that question
on a regular basis. Why? Because the reason we are given influence or dominion at all is for the flourishing of others. Dominion and influence are given so that the kingdom of God can grow
by filling the earth with the knowledge of God and his Word. As
this happens, disciples are made.

Who are we to be? Image bearers. What happens when we
do this well? We bring the rule and reign of God to bear and the
kingdom of God advances, filling the whole earth. As a result,
people are blessed and all of creation flourishes. One of the most

amazing aspects of this is that God is at work repairing, redeeming, and restoring what man broke (remember Genesis 3). And instead of pushing man aside and saying, "Get out of my way; I'm having to fix what you broke," he calls us back into his work and entrusts us again with his mission. He is a God of grace, a God who redeems us even as he is using us in his mission of redeeming all things.

This mandate to mission should cause us to ask these questions: How do I participate, where do I go, and what do I do? If the call is to fill the earth and be a blessing to all peoples, then we need to know what areas of life need to be redeemed. So we ask, What areas of life have been stained by sin? Has business been affected by sin? Politics? Art? Families? Education? Absolutely, on every count! And the list is endless. So where does God send his people? Into all areas!

Jesus said in Mark 16:15, "Go into all the world and proclaim the gospel to the whole creation." That is our calling—where to go and what to do. But how do we do it?

I like how Amy Sherman explains it in her book *Kingdom Calling*. She tells of a time that Jeff White came to her church:

> He talked about the work of King Jesus in bringing restoration and held up one of those tiny pink taste-test spoons from Baskin-Robbins. You know, the spoons that offer you a foretaste of the ice cream to come. Jeff challenged attendees to see themselves as such spoons, for our role in the world is about offering foretastes of the kingdom to our neighbors near and far.[5]

Going back to what my professor asked me: Who is flourishing because of the influence and dominion you have been given? In what ways might you be a tiny pink taste-test spoon of the gospel to those around you? Let God use you to fill the earth with the knowledge and worship of him.

GO AND BE A BLESSING

> Now the LORD said to Abram, "Go...and I will bless you and make your name great, so that you will be a blessing...and in you all the families of the earth shall be blessed" (Genesis 12:1-3).

If we had to summarize God's command to Abraham in Genesis 12:1-3, it would be this: "Go and be a blessing." Or, as Chris Wright says, "go" for the purpose of being a blessing.[6] In chapter 4, we looked at the importance of the phrase "so that"; God called Abraham *so that* he would be a blessing. And just whom was God going to bless through Abraham? No less than all the families of the earth.

Has that happened? Partially. If you are in Christ, you and I are part of the glorious fulfillment of God accomplishing what he set out to do through Abraham! We are among the people who have been blessed through Abraham. And, one day, the fullness of God's mission will be complete as we worship around the throne with "every nation and tribe and language and people" (Revelation 14:6)—people from all the families of the earth. But remember where we are in the story; it is not finished, and we have a part to play. Understanding the call for Abraham is key to our understanding the call on our lives. We, too, are called to go and be a blessing.

Go: Where was Abraham called to go? He was called to leave his country, family, and home. But he wasn't merely called *from* something, he was called *to* something—to the land God would show him. He was called to walk away and walk toward. He was called out and he was called in—he was set apart for God's purposes.

What about us? Have we been called out and set apart? Have

you been called from and called to? Have you been called to walk away and walk toward? You and I may not be called to leave family, home, or country (although we might be), but as Christians, we are called to walk away from our former ways of life. Scripture tells us that we have been transferred from our former home, the domain of darkness, into a new place, the kingdom of Christ (Colossians 1:13). We have been called out to follow God and called into the things of God.

It is important to note that God did not call Abraham because of anything good or righteous he had done. God called Abraham because God chose to call Abraham—based solely on God's sovereign, free initiative and will. The same is true for us. We do not earn or merit the salvation of the Lord; he calls us his own because he has chosen to do so. But, like Abraham, that call requires a response; it requires obedience. For Abraham, he had to get up, put some clothes in a bag, saddle a donkey or two, and start walking. For us, we need to get up and start putting off a few things and putting on some others. Obedience matters.

> Put to death therefore what is earthly in you: sexual immorality, impurity, passion, evil desire, and covetousness, which is idolatry…But now you must put them all away: anger, wrath, malice, slander, and obscene talk from your mouth. Do not lie to one another, seeing that you have put off the old self with its practices and have put on the new self, which is being renewed in knowledge after the image of its creator…Put on then, as God's chosen ones, holy and beloved, compassionate hearts, kindness, humility, meekness, and patience…And above all these put on love, which binds everything together in perfect harmony (Colossians 3:5, 8-10, 12, 14).

If Abraham was to be the blessing to others that he was called to be—if he was to be the faithful participant in God's mission that he was supposed to be—he had to be obedient. The same is true for us. Our obedience directly affects our ability to be faithful participants in the story. We cannot be a blessing if we are not obedient.

To understand how and where we are to be a blessing, we must understand what exactly it means to be a blessing. We can bless people with our words, our actions, our time, and our resources. But what kind of blessing is Genesis 12 calling us to be? Wright links the command in Genesis 12—*go and be a blessing so that all the families of the earth will be blessed*—directly to the command in Matthew 28—*go and make disciples in all nations.*[7] The call on our lives to be a blessing has to involve calling others to know and worship the God of Abraham because ultimately, we know that "in Christ alone, through the gospel of his death and resurrection, stands the hope of blessing for all nations."[8]

> You have been called out, set apart, and blessed. And both your calling out and your blessings are essential to the part you play in the unfolding drama all around you.

We are a blessing as we go, teach, explain, disciple, proclaim, and live the gospel to and with others. We do this through our words, actions, time, and resources. We take all of what we have been given and "bring it to the table," so to speak, of blessing others. As God told Abraham, you have been blessed so that you will be a blessing.

Our blessings come in many shapes and sizes, but bless us, God does. The call of Abraham is our call too. Our salvation is never for our sake alone. We are saved and then called to be mediators of that salvation to others. We get to be the vehicle God uses to take his salvation to those around us. You have been called out, set apart, and blessed. And both your calling out and your blessings are essential to the part you play in the unfolding drama all around you. You are not in the audience; you have been called into the spotlight and equipped with the blessings needed to play your part.

HOLINESS MATTERS

> I am the LORD who brought you up out of the land of Egypt to be your God. *You shall therefore be holy, for I am holy* (Leviticus 11:45, emphasis added).

In this chapter, we are looking back through the story to see how it informs the way we are to live. We are participants in this story, actors in the great drama, and if we want to be faithful to the storyline (and not like someone reciting *Hamlet* in the middle of *The Lion King*), then we need to know the trajectory of the story.

We have seen over and over that God called his people to be a holy people. How are we to bear God's image? We must be holy. How are we to be a blessing to all the families of the earth? We must be holy.

Holiness involves the concept of being set apart as well as the idea of being ethically and morally righteous. The call to be holy is a call to be set apart, to live our lives differently. We are to be characterized by the pursuit of traits that display holiness— righteousness, justice, kindness, and humility.

We tend to think of holiness in one of two ways: either it doesn't matter because we are saved by grace, or we view it as the end goal of the Christian life. Neither of these is correct. Holiness matters— it always has. Both our personal holiness and our corporate holiness in the church are of vital importance. But our holiness serves the greater purpose of the mission of God. Our holiness says as much about God as it does about us. What kind of people are we to be? Holy. Why? Because we serve a holy God.

Remember, the book of Leviticus contains rules and regulations about ritual cleansing and purity. These rules were given to the people so they would know how to approach the holy God who was now living in their midst. It is a book that loudly proclaims both the holiness of God and the need for God's people to be holy. It is set in the context of both the kingdom and mission of God. What does God's kingdom look like? It is a kingdom with a holy king and holy subjects (Exodus 19:6: "You shall be to me a kingdom of priests and a holy nation"). How does that holiness serve the mission of God? It displays holiness to a watching world, and it ought to cause others to want to know this good, righteous, and holy King (review Deuteronomy 4:5-8).

If we want to know how we are to live the moments, days, weeks, and years of our lives in a way that is consistent with the story we are in, we have to understand that our holiness matters. One of the first ways we learn to faithfully stick to the script is to recognize that we are to live as holy people. Anything else is not consistent with the storyline. At some level, we all know this is true. We say things like, "Don't talk the talk if you're not going to walk the walk." Or we grimace in sadness when a pastor or spiritual leader fails morally. We know that there should be a consistency between what we profess and how we act—we are to watch both our life and our doctrine closely (1 Timothy 4:16).

But, even when we are convinced holiness matters, do we understand the far-reaching, missional aspect of our holiness? Many of us tend to think (at least I know I did!) that our individual pursuit of holiness is a matter "between God and me." But it is so much greater. Wright says the call to holiness for Israel (and subsequently, for us) "was not merely for their (our) own good or even merely to keep God happy."⁹ Both of those aspects are true, but that is not all! Peter wrote:

> You are a chosen race, a royal priesthood, a holy nation, a people for his own possession, that you may proclaim the excellencies of him who called you out of darkness into his marvelous light. Once you were not a people, but now you are God's people; once you had not received mercy, but now you have received mercy.
>
> Beloved, I urge you as sojourners and exiles to abstain from the passions of the flesh, which wage war against your soul. Keep your conduct among the Gentiles honorable, so that when they speak against you as evildoers, they may see your good deeds and glorify God on the day of visitation (1 Peter 2:9-12).

We are a holy people *so that* we can proclaim God's excellencies. Our holy conduct can cause unbelievers to glorify God! The verses immediately before these tell us that we are living stones being built into a holy dwelling place. And, as we have seen, the glory of the Lord now dwells in you and me, individually as well as corporately. I am a temple of the living God; you are a temple of the living God. But most importantly, we are the temple of the living God. As Sandra Richter says:

> The Presence from which Adam and Eve were driven, that rested on Mt. Sinai with thunder and storm, that sat enthroned above the cherubim, now resides in you. It is nearly too much to apprehend. And just as the old covenant Temple housed the Presence in order to make God available to saint and sinner alike and stood as a testimony to the nations that Yahweh dwelt among his

people, so too the church. You and I, and we as the church, are designed to be that place which believer and unbeliever can come to find God. Moreover, our restored lives are God's testimony to the nations that he lives and dwells among us. And whereas the Temple was one building that could only be in one place, the church is an ever-expanding community that is slowly, steadily bringing the Presence to the farthest reaches of the world.[10]

Do you see what Richter is saying? Our holiness serves as a testimony to both the power and presence of the Lord. And God is now using us, as those he has made holy, to mediate his presence—his holy presence—to the world.

We pray, "Your kingdom come." And as we do, we must realize that the kingdom comes only when people acknowledge and reflect God's holiness. If God's holiness is not present in his people, his kingdom is not present in that place. That is why our holiness matters; it's why we must be holy as he is holy.

Points to Remember from Chapter 9

- We each have a part to play in the story, and our "scene" is now!

- We are being conformed into the image of Christ so that we can be accurate image bearers in all areas of life.

- The mission of God has always been to fill the earth with his presence by filling the earth with image bearers who know and worship him.

- Dominion, authority, and influence are given to us to fill the earth with the presence of God.

- We are blessed so that we will be a blessing to others.
- Our holiness matters.

Discussion Questions

1. In what ways does knowing more about God's story of redemption help you understand what part you have to play?

2. What has God used in your life to conform you to his image? In what ways are you currently being conformed?

3. List two or three areas in which the Lord might be calling you to be obedient. They could be things you are to walk away from or things you are to walk into, things you are to put off or things you are to put on, places you are to leave or places you are to go.

4. Read Galatians 5:22-23. What fruit are we to bear? How do you think bearing fruit and image bearing are connected?

5. In what ways is the gospel increasing and bearing fruit in your life?

6. Who is flourishing because of your dominion?

7. In what ways are you currently participating in God's mission by being fruitful and multiplying (making disciples)?

8. Read Mark 16:15. What is the scope of the mission Jesus gives his disciples? What are some areas to which you have been sent on God's mission to redeem all things? In what ways can you faithfully play your part?

9. Either write below or share with your group one point, truth, or lesson that either challenged or encouraged you from this chapter.

For Further Study

1. Looking at Genesis 1:27-28 and Genesis 12:3, write down some of the ways the commission given in Matthew 28:18-20 is a reissuing of these two previous commissions.

2. Read John 17:18. Jesus says that the Father sent him. In light of Genesis 12:1-3, how does this make Jesus the even greater Abraham?

3. Read 2 Corinthians 6:16–7:1 and answer the following:

   • What does God call us (verse 16)?

   • What is the covenantal phrase God uses?

- What command is given in verse 17?

- What is the only appropriate response (7:1)?

- What are you doing in your life to "bring holiness to completion"?

4. Read Ephesians 4:22-32. Using the chart below, list everything Paul says to put off (or walk away from) and put on (or walk into). Which do you need to do today?

Put off/walk away from	Put on/walk into

CHAPTER 10

HAPPILY EVER AFTER

Scripture Memory

"He who was seated on the throne said, 'Behold, I am making all things new.' Also he said, 'Write this down, for these words are trustworthy and true'" (Revelation 21:5).

Pray

"God so loved the world, that he gave his only Son, that whoever believes in him should not perish but have eternal life" (John 3:16). Father, thank you for loving me, for sending your Son, and for, through Jesus, making a way for me to live with you forever. Help me to rest in your amazing love.

What does a good ending to a good story look like? To reference *Tangled* one last time, we know that a good and right conclusion to that story involved Rapunzel being restored to the same kingdom from which she was taken, returned to the same parents from which she was stolen—not to new parents or to a different kingdom. We know that a good and right conclusion requires the restoration of all that was declared good and right in the beginning. The ending is tied to the beginning. Our story is no different. We will now look at what will be new about heaven, and what parts of the story we can anticipate finding in heaven!

Heaven is not some ethereal site disconnected from the story. It is not a separate place that is new and utterly different from the first creation of God. Instead, heaven is where the story is made complete; it is the perfect renewal of the creation and the place in which we were created to dwell. It is the completion of all that God began in Eden. The only way for this story to be brought to its intended and glorious conclusion—for us to experience the "happily ever after" that our hearts long for—is for all things to be

> We need to understand what we can about heaven for two reasons: so that our hope will increase, and so that our actions would more consistently reflect our hope.

fulfilled, restored, and made right. But, for some reason, we tend to detach our hopes and thoughts about heaven from the rest of the story.

When one of our sons was around seven years old, he announced from the back seat of our minivan that he didn't want to go to heaven when he died. I quickly looked in the rearview mirror and asked him why. He gazed at me with deep sincerity and said that he did not want to "sit around all day in a choir robe and sing."

That was how he pictured life in heaven, and to a seven-year-old boy, that sounded like no fun at all. His view and understanding of heaven affected his desire (or lack thereof) to be there. And if his view had remained (it didn't), eventually his actions would have reflected his lack of hope. Why? Because our understanding of the future affects our hopes for the future, and our hopes for the future shape our behavior in the present.

We need to understand what we can about heaven for two

reasons: so that our hope will increase, and so that our actions would more consistently reflect our hope. We need consistency between what we believe and how we live.

FIRST THINGS FIRST

When we talk about heaven, we must understand that there is heaven now—the place where all believers who die before Jesus comes again go immediately. This place is called the intermediate heaven, and it is glorious. Remember what Jesus told the thief on the cross next to him? "Truly, I say to you, *today* you will be with me in *paradise*" (Luke 23:43, emphasis added). Or what Paul said in Philippians: "For to me to live is Christ, and to die is gain…I am hard pressed between the two. My desire is to depart and *be with Christ, for that is far better*" (Philippians 1:21, 23).

Every believer who has already died or who will die before Jesus comes again (see 1 Thessalonians 4:16-17; Revelation 21:1-5) is in this paradise with Jesus right now. But, as good as the current heaven is, the eternal heaven will be even more glorious!

For the rest of this chapter, we will be discussing the eternal heaven, the place where all believers will dwell with God for all eternity.

ALL THINGS NEW

> I saw a new heaven and a new earth, for the first heaven and the first earth had passed away, and the sea was no more (Revelation 21:1).

What images come to mind when you think of heaven? I remember a picture that was in my white leather Bible with a zipper. Heaven, according to this picture, was a place in the clouds with white castles, angels in white robes, a surreal sun with rays going in every direction, and a big brass gate at the entrance. It looked more like the place my seven-year-old son was hoping to avoid than the place I see portrayed in the Bible.

Heaven will be more glorious than we can imagine, but God gives us glimpses of it in Scripture. We are informed of what the world was like when all was as it was supposed to be, and we are told what the world will look like when all things have been made new. And the first informs the second. Our final destination will not be a completely new and different place; it will be a renewed creation. God will not toss out his original creation and start over; he will redeem and restore what he originally made. How do we know? The Bible tells us so.

In Romans 8:18-25, Paul explained that all of creation—everything that was called into existence in Genesis 1—is waiting, groaning even, for redemption. And that redemption (verse 23) will somehow be like the redemption of our bodies. To understand the redemption of our bodies (and therefore of all creation), we need only to look at the resurrected body we know—the body of the resurrected Jesus (when I say that, I mean resurrected not to the same type of mortal body like Lazarus was, but to an immortal body!).

There was both continuity and discontinuity between Jesus's pre-resurrection body and his post-resurrection body. Some aspects of him were the same, while others were changed. He was both recognizable (John 20:19-20) and unrecognizable (John 20:15). His first body was perishable, corruptible, and mortal; his second imperishable, incorruptible, and eternal. But it was *his* body that was resurrected—not a brand new, totally different body. The body that went into the tomb was the body that came out of the tomb. What Paul was telling us in Romans 8 is that not just our bodies, but *all* of creation will experience this same glorious redemption.

When John was given a glimpse of the glorious, anticipated

climax of our story, he wrote, "I saw a new heaven and a new earth, for the first heaven and the first earth had passed away, and the sea was no more" (Revelation 21:1) At first glance, it looks as if John was telling us that the first heaven and earth will be pushed out of the way, and that we will be in a brand new heaven and earth.

But what's wrong with this understanding? First, we know that scripture does not contradict scripture. Paul told us that all of creation is eagerly waiting for the redemption that will be like the redemption of our bodies. Anthony Hoekema writes:

> Those raised with Christ will not be a totally new set of human beings, but the people of God who have lived on this earth. By way of analogy, we would expect that the new earth will not be totally different from the present earth but will be the present earth wondrously renewed.[1]

So what did John mean when he wrote that he saw a new heaven and a new earth? Michael Williams says, "New means new in quality rather than new in time or origin."[2] Albert Wolters explains that God does not give up on his creation: "[God] hangs onto his fallen original creation and salvages it. He refuses to abandon the work of his hands—in fact, he sacrifices his own Son to save his original project."[3]

And this makes sense with the rest of the story. God is going to renew his people and his creation. Randy Alcorn says,

> God has never given up on his original creation. Yet somehow, we have managed to overlook an entire biblical vocabulary that makes this point clear. Reconcile. Redeem. Restore. Recover. Return. Renew. Regenerate. Resurrect. Each of these biblical words begins with the re- prefix, suggesting a return to an original condition that was ruined or lost.[4]

My husband did not become a believer until his early adult years, which is why the truth of 2 Corinthians 5:17 is particularly dear to him. Paul wrote, "if anyone is in Christ, he is a new creation. The old has passed away; behold, the new has come." The word "new" is the same one used in Revelation 21. In the same way that we are not done away with, but our original self is made new, so will it be with the new heavens and new earth. God will renew his original creation, not make a brand-new creation. That which God called very good in the beginning will be made very, very good in the end.

You might be saying, "So what? What difference does it make?" For starters, this informs how we are to live here. How many times have you heard, "This world is not my home"? Well, actually it is! Not in its present form—we have said over and over that things are not the way they should be. This world currently suffers under the curse. It is a tough place in which to work, produce, and profit—it is by the sweat of our brow that we labor. And it is in this world that we experience sin, suffering, tears, shame, and death. Remember, none of those things were part of the original creation. Looking back to Eden gives us a glimpse of what we can anticipate, but looking forward to glory, we see that everything will be even better because God is making it anew.

Understanding that God is in the business of restoring all his good creation has changed the way I view the world. I love it more. I pause and appreciate more the beauty of a harvest moon. I delight more when I jump into the lake and feel the delight of cold water on a hot summer day. I worship God as I ride my horse through a misty forest and feel the cool breeze on my face. I look around me and rejoice that the beauty of this place—my home—will be both redeemed and be mine forever and forever.

Understanding the cosmic scope of redemption also changes

the way we view God. His creation is not just some nuisance to him. He loves what he made, and that includes you and me. He has been working to save us, not get rid of us and start over. The more I realize this, the more I rest in his love.

THE TREE OF LIFE

> The angel showed me the river of the water of life, bright as crystal, flowing from the throne of God and of the Lamb through the middle of the street of the city; also, on either side of the river, the tree of life with its twelve kinds of fruit, yielding its fruit each month. The leaves of the tree were for the healing of the nations (Revelation 22:1-2).

In March 2014, my mom and I took my two daughters to Florida for their spring break—first to Disney World, and then to the beach. We decided to take a day trip and drive to Saint Augustine, a small and beautiful town on the northeast coast of Florida. Saint Augustine is famed for being one of the oldest Spanish settlements in the United States. It is also known for being the home to the highly sought after (and supposed) fountain of youth. My mom and I were, of course, very interested in finding this fountain! We did, and yet it has proven to be less than magical. My hair has continued to gray, new wrinkles seem to show up every morning, my mother's arthritis has continued to plague her, and there seems to be no end to our aches and pains.

One of the realities of this world is that we age, and our bodies slowly wind down. And yet, so many of us fight aging; we know deep within our souls that the effects of aging are not what God intended. So we look in all kinds of places for weapons with which to fight this enemy—everything from the fountain of youth to the fountain of new medical breakthroughs. We exercise, take vitamins, buy the latest face serum, and dye our hair. Some go so far as to surgically remove or alter the signs, hoping that, before it's too late, someone will discover "the cure" for this horrible disease called aging.

The reason we long for a fountain of youth is because we were created for it! Remember what was in the center of the garden? The tree of life, given so Adam and Eve (and any who had access to it) would have immortality. The tree of life was the true Fountain of Youth—take of it, and you will never die. This is why our hearts long for immortality, but, like the song says about looking for love, we search for it in all the wrong places.

Where should we look? The last chapter in the Bible begins with these words:

> The angel showed me the river of the water of life, bright as crystal, flowing from the throne of God and of the Lamb through the middle of the street of the city; also, on either side of the river, the tree of life with its twelve kinds of fruit, yielding its fruit each month. The leaves of the tree were for the healing of the nations (Revelation 22:1-2).

The tree of life will be waiting for us in the new heavens and new earth!

T. Desmond Alexander explains:

> In keeping with its designation, the tree of life produces fruit that gives immortality...Citizens of the new earth will experience and enjoy both wholeness of body and longevity of life. They will have a quality of life unrestricted by disability or disease. To live in

the New Jerusalem is to experience life in all its fullness and vitality. It is to live as one has never lived before. It is to be in the prime of life, for the whole of one's life.[5]

Do you see what Alexander is saying? The things we long and strive for—health, wholeness, longevity—will be ours because we will once again have access to the tree of life. We will experience the complete healing of our minds, hearts, and bodies—no more depression, disease, anxiety, arthritis, cavities, congestive heart failure, sinus infections, strokes, migraines, or any of the myriad things that plague us.

God's mercy compelled him to expel Adam and Eve from the first garden. If he hadn't, they would have lived in their new state of sin and misery forever. And God loves us too much to leave us in that state. In fact, the entire story of redemption is the story of the great lengths to which God goes to ensure that we don't live in that state forever, but to bring us again into a state of holiness and allow us to live forever in his presence.

So how will we have access to the tree of life again? The answer is so beautiful I can barely take it in. Acts 5:30 says, "The God of our fathers raised Jesus, whom you killed by hanging him on a tree." God brings us back to the tree by way of another tree. It was mercy that kept us from having access to the first tree of life, and mercy that takes us back to the tree again—all through the work of the tree of death. The cross was an instrument of death, but it brings us again to the tree of life. That is the paradox of the gospel—life (ours) through death (Christ's).

As we set our hopes on heaven, know for certain that the Lord is returning us to that which we were created for: life, health, holiness, and wholeness. He will wash away every sin; he will deliver us completely from the penalty, power, and presence of sin. And then—and only then—will he give us access to the tree of life. And we will live forever.

THE THRONE OF GOD

> At once I was in the Spirit, and behold, a throne stood in heaven, with one seated on the throne (Revelation 4:2).

At the center of any kingdom is the palace, and at the center of any palace is the throne room, and the center of any throne room is the throne. Now, there is a vast difference between walking into a throne room with an empty throne and into one where the king is seated on the throne. That is because ultimately, a kingdom, a palace, a throne room, and a throne are all about the one who sits on the throne. The kingdom is always about the king, and the kingdom of God is no different.

In some ways, this story has been all about the throne—or, more accurately, the one seated on the throne. God has eternally been on a throne ruling over a kingdom that encompasses all of heaven and earth. But our access to that throne has varied. Our story began with Adam and Eve, the children of the King, having full access to their Father. They walked with him in broad daylight—so much so that they knew the sound of his footsteps. But when they were exiled from the garden, they no longer had access to the presence of the King. And as the story moved forward from that point, we have seen that one of the glorious aspects of God's redemptive plan is that he works to grant access to his children again!

But the restoration of access has been gradual. Remember when God established the tabernacle? We looked briefly at how the tabernacle was more than a mere tent in the desert; it was a palace for the King. The Holy of Holies served as the throne room of God, where he chose to be enthroned above the cherubim

(2 Samuel 6:2). And his glory filled the place! It is worth pausing for a moment and remembering that this earthly throne room in no way meant that God's eternal throne had been abdicated.

But through the tabernacle (and later the temple), God began the process of granting access to his throne room once again. However, it was far from full access. Do you remember all the sacrifices, rituals, and offerings that had to be carried out? Do you remember that only one man, the high priest, could enter the Holy of Holies? And that this one man could enter the throne room only once a year? That was a far cry from the access that Adam and Eve had in Eden. But it was the mercy of our King that prevented full access. We have to remember that coming into the presence of an earthly king is frightening, and coming into the presence of the holy, eternal, divine King is even more terrifying.

Consider Isaiah's reaction when he was given a glimpse of the King on his throne:

> In the year that King Uzziah died I saw the Lord sitting upon a throne, high and lifted up; and the train of his robe filled the temple. Above him stood the seraphim. Each had six wings: with two he covered his face, and with two he covered his feet, and with two he flew. And one called to another and said: "Holy, holy, holy is the LORD of hosts; the whole earth is full of his glory!" And the foundations of the thresholds shook at the voice of him who called, and the house was filled with smoke. And I said: "Woe is me! For I am lost; for I am a man of unclean lips, and I dwell in the midst of a people of unclean lips; for my eyes have seen the King, the LORD of hosts!" (Isaiah 6:1-5).

The interjection "woe" is an utterance of fear, grief, anguish, and despair. Isaiah was crying out in shock because he was in a place that would completely undo him—he was sure he could not see what he was seeing and live. He experienced the terror of the unholy coming into the presence of the Holy. And this is the terror we should feel at the thought that we will one day be ushered into the throne room, before the throne, and into the presence of the one seated on it. That is to say, if we are ushered before God on our own.

We cannot stand before the throne of God in the filth of our sin and misery. We would not survive. And yet our Father-King longed for us to be ushered back into his presence. So the rightful heir to the throne removed his crown, took off his royal robes, and stepped down. He took on our filth and gave us his purity. And those things he took off—his crown and his royal robes—he then put on us so that he can freely bring us back into the throne room, before the throne, and ultimately, before the one seated on the throne. We can stand in that place only if we are clothed in Christ himself.

In Revelation 7 we read,

> After this I looked, and behold, a great multitude that no one could number, from every nation, from all tribes and peoples and languages, standing before the throne and before the Lamb, clothed in white robes, with palm branches in their hands, and crying out with a loud voice, "Salvation belongs to our God who sits on the throne, and to the Lamb!"…Then one of the elders addressed me, saying, "Who are these, clothed in white robes, and from where have they come?" I said to him, "Sir, you know." And he said to me, "These are the ones coming out of the great tribulation. They have washed

their robes and made them white in the blood of the Lamb. Therefore they are before the throne of God, and serve him day and night in his temple; and he who sits on the throne will shelter them with his presence. They shall hunger no more, neither thirst anymore; the sun shall not strike them, nor any scorching heat. For the Lamb in the midst of the throne will be their shepherd, and he will guide them to springs of living water, and God will wipe away every tear from their eyes" (Revelation 7:9-10, 13-17).

We will one day stand before the throne and our cry will not be "Woe is me," but rather, "Worthy is he." Second Corinthians 5:21 says that "for our sake he made him to be sin who knew no sin, so that in him we might become the righteousness of God." You see, if we are clothed in the righteousness of Christ, we no longer have to cry out, "Woe is me." Instead, we will be free to stand before the throne of God—the place we were created to be—and do that which we were created to do: fall on our faces and worship so great a King. We will be able to stand before him, and instead of being consumed by him, we will be sheltered by him.

But what about now? What access do we have today? Do we have more access than the Israelites who worshipped in the tabernacle or temple? Yes. Are we to feel utter despair like Isaiah felt until we reach heaven? No. The writer of Hebrews tells us,

Since then we have a great high priest who has passed through the heavens, Jesus, the Son of God, let us hold fast our confession. For we do not have a high priest who is unable to sympathize with our weaknesses, but one who in every respect has been tempted as we are,

yet without sin. Let us then with confidence draw near
to the throne of grace, that we may receive mercy and
find grace to help in time of need (4:14-16).

We will one day be granted such full and complete access that
I believe we will know what the footsteps of our King sound like.
We will know the sound of his voice and even know the beauty of
his face. But until then, we have had a great and final high priest
offer the great and final sacrifice. As a result, we can now draw
near to the throne of grace—and we will receive mercy and help
from the one seated on the throne.

THE DWELLING OF GOD

I heard a loud voice from the throne saying, "Behold,
the dwelling place of God is with man. He will dwell
with them, and they will be his people, and God himself will be with them as their God" (Revelation 21:3).

Out of all that was lost when Adam and Eve were expelled
from the garden, there is one loss that stands out as greater than
the rest: Adam and Eve lost the ability to dwell with their Father
and he with them. Early on, we looked at the heart of God and
his desire to be with his people: "I will be your God, you will be
my people, and I will dwell with you" is the heartbeat of our God.
This has been the main thread of our story. It began in the garden and has moved the entire story forward. The great dilemma
in our story is that a holy and faithful God longs to dwell with
his people; however, they (we) are unholy and unfaithful, and a
holy God cannot dwell in the midst of the unholy. But God has
been moving and acting, promising and fulfilling, and dying and
rising again in order to accomplish his plan and solve the great

dilemma. And, along the way, we have seen him progressively advance toward his goal.

The tabernacle and the temple were God's way of drawing near to his people. But, as Sandra Richter pointed out, both drew attention to the "agony of redemptive history."[6] That is, both the tabernacle and the temple showed God's people that he wanted to dwell among them, but the complicated system of sacrifices, offerings, and rituals reminded them that he couldn't fully dwell with them lest they die.

But in Revelation 21, we read, "I saw no temple in the city, for its temple is the Lord God the Almighty and the Lamb" (verse 22). As wonderful as the tabernacle

> The Author of this story knows every hair on your head. He treasures you, made you with a purpose, loves you, and is longing to dwell fully with you for all time.

and the temple were, they fell short of the fullness of the glory that comes with truly dwelling with God. In the new heavens and new earth, we will see the Lord as he is (1 John 3:2). We will walk with him again in the cool of the day (Genesis 3:8). We will be able to speak with him face to face (Exodus 33:11; 1 Corinthians 13:12). The Lord himself will be our temple.

In Jesus's incarnation, we have been given a foretaste of what this will be like. While in human flesh, he walked with his people and sat with them face to face. Jesus said that anyone who had seen him had seen the Father (John 14:9). But that was just a foretaste because the disciples were still sinful people, the world was still under the curse, and Jesus's presence on earth was limited geographically and temporally. However, when we dwell with the Almighty and the Lamb in the new heavens and new earth, our cleansing will be complete, our veils will have been lifted, and our access will be unlimited. Oh, what a glorious ending to an amazing story!

And so the story ends, but what a story it is! From the garden to glory, God has a plan. Richter says, "At the end of all things, God is once again with his people. Access to the Presence is restored. Adam has returned to the garden. Redemption has been accomplished."[7]

This story encompasses all of creation and every life that has ever been. And, at the same time, the Author of this story knows every hair on your head. He treasures you, made you with a purpose, loves you, and is longing to dwell fully with you for all time. He is working all things together for your good and the good of his people. And he is calling you to take your place in this glorious story. His story is meant to change your story.

So, until that day when we stand together before the throne, worship him, follow him, and proclaim him. He is worthy!

PRAY

> The grace of God has appeared, bringing salvation for all people, training us to renounce ungodliness and worldly passions, and to live self-controlled, upright, and godly lives in the present age, waiting for our blessed hope, the appearing of the glory of our great God and Savior Jesus Christ (Titus 2:11-13).

If you are a believer, pray:

> *Father, thank you for sending Jesus to accomplish such a great a salvation. Thank you for making me part of your people. May I serve your kingdom all the days of my life,*

obeying your good Word, and living according to your holy will.

If you are not a believer and would like to be, pray:

Father, I believe that you sent your Son, Jesus, to rescue me. I believe that by your Spirit I can be born again and, as a result, will live with you forever. I confess my sin and my need of a Savior. Today, I put all my hope and faith on Jesus as the one and only Savior of the world. Thank you that you are faithful and good. Let me rest in all your good promises and live out your glorious gospel of grace.

Points to Remember from Chapter 10

- The story of our redemption stretches from the garden to the new heavens and new earth.

- God sits on an eternal throne, and we will one day be ushered back into his throne room to stand before him who is seated on the throne.

- Because of Jesus, all that was good and right in the garden will be ours again, including the tree of life, access to the throne room, and intimacy with the one seated on the throne.

- The story of the Bible is one plot line: God is redeeming and restoring his creation.

- The story is not over until we are once again dwelling with God and he with us.

- From the garden to glory, our God is a God to be worshipped and adored.

Discussion Questions

1. Share with your group (or write down) some of the good parts of this world that will endure and how you anticipate enjoying them forever.

2. How does the fact that God loves and is redeeming all of his creation cause you to think about how God views you?

3. What do you think your response will be when you are ushered into the throne room and stand before the one seated on his throne?

4. Read Philippians 2:5-8. Using the imagery of the throne room from Isaiah 6, describe what Christ removed, what he stepped down from, and what he left behind.

5. Read Hebrews 12:1-2. Why did Jesus do what Philippians 2 says he did? Are there areas of your own life in which you currently need to be reminded of the joy set before you so that you, like Jesus, can persevere?

6. Read Revelation 5:9-10. What has the Lamb made the ransomed people to be (verse 10)? Where have you seen that before?

7. Think back to the young man we talked about in the introduction, the one who didn't think *The Passion* had much of a plot. How would you now answer him?

8. At the end of chapter 1, you had the opportunity to write a summary of the Bible's story. Write another summary now and compare the two. How does your new summary differ from the previous one?

9. Read Revelation 21:4. Who will be wiping away your tears? What will be no more? What does this verse tell us about what life will be like when we dwell with our very good, very loving Father?

10. Either write below or share with your group one point, truth, or lesson that either challenged or encouraged you from this chapter.

For Further Study

1. Compare Genesis 2:8-10 with Revelation 22:1-5 (see below). Underline the words that show the continuity between the tree in the garden and the tree in the new garden.

Genesis 2:8-10	Revelation 22:1-5
The LORD God planted a garden in Eden, in the east, and there he put the man whom he had formed. And out of the ground the LORD God made to spring up every tree that is pleasant to the sight and good for food. The tree of life was in the midst of the garden, and the tree of the knowledge of good and evil. A river flowed out of Eden to water the garden, and there it divided and became four rivers.	The angel showed me the river of the water of life, bright as crystal, flowing from the throne of God and of the Lamb through the middle of the street of the city; also, on either side of the river, the tree of life with its twelve kinds of fruit, yielding its fruit each month. The leaves of the tree were for the healing of the nations. No longer will there be anything accursed, but the throne of God and of the Lamb will be in it, and his servants will worship him. They will see his face, and his name will be on their foreheads. And night will be no more. They will need no light of lamp or sun, for the Lord God will be their light, and they will reign forever and ever.

2. Among the questions people ask about heaven are these: Where is heaven? If it is not going to be a totally new place, where is it now? Where should we fix our eyes and set our hope? I find Michael Williams, once again, to be most helpful:

> At present, because Christ is ascended to the Father in heaven, heaven is the sphere of the present fulfillment of the promise of salvation. Andrew Lincoln appropriately writes, "Because Christ has been exalted to heaven, heaven rather than earth temporarily provides the chief focus for salvation and for the believer's orientation until Christ's coming from heaven when salvation will then embrace heaven and earth...This earth is not our home until Jesus comes, brings heaven with him, and makes all things new."[8]

Remember, in the beginning, God created the heavens and the earth (Genesis 1:1). In Revelation 21:1-2, what does John see coming down? Nothing less than the new heavens and new earth. So where is heaven? It is the place where God the Father and God the Son sit enthroned—because heaven is all about them. For now, heaven is the place where they currently sit. But one day, that throne and kingdom will come down and encompass both heaven and earth.

- Use your sanctified imagination to write a description of what your life might be like on the new earth.

- Make a list of words that come to mind as you dream about what this life will be like. What one aspect of this life do you most long for?

3. Read Leviticus 26:11-12. Take a minute to trace and explain the unfolding of the promise in verse 12 ("I will walk among you") throughout the story. In other words, where in the story have you seen the promise become a reality? Name as many places as you can think of.

MEMORY VERSE CHALLENGE

2 Peter 1:21—

Genesis 1:31—

Genesis 3:15—

Leviticus 26:12—

Exodus 19:5-6—

2 Samuel 7:16—

Matthew 1:23—

Acts 4:12—

Matthew 28:18-20—

Revelation 21:5—

BIBLIOGRAPHY

Alcorn, Randy C. *Heaven*. Wheaton, IL: Tyndale, 2004.

Alexander, T. Desmond. *From Eden to the New Jerusalem: An Introduction to Biblical Theology*. Grand Rapids, MI: Kregel Academic & Professional, 2009, 2008.

——. *From Paradise to the Promised Land: An Introduction to the Pentateuch*. 2nd ed. Cambria, UK: Paternoster Press, 2002.

Barber, Dan C. and Robert A. Peterson. *Life Everlasting: The Unfolding Story of Heaven*. Phillipsburg, NJ: P&R, 2012.

Beale, G.K. *God Dwells Among Us: Expanding Eden to the Ends of the Earth*. Downers Grove, IL: InterVarsity, 2014.

——. and D.A. Carson, eds. *Commentary on the New Testament Use of the Old Testament*. Grand Rapids, MI: Baker Academic, 2007.

Collins, C. John. *Did Adam and Eve Really Exist? Who They Were and Why You Should Care*. Wheaton, IL: Crossway, 2011.

——. *Genesis 1–4: A Linguistic, Literary, and Theological Commentary*. Phillipsburg, NJ: P&R, 2006.

——. *Science and Faith: Friends or Foes?* Wheaton, IL: Crossway, 2003.

Ferguson, Sinclair B. *The Holy Spirit. Contours of Christian Theology*. Downers Grove, IL: InterVarsity, 1996.

Hoekema, Anthony A. *The Bible and the Future*. Grand Rapids, MI: Eerdmans, 1979.

Keil, Carl Friedrich and Franz Delitzsch. *Commentary On the Old Testament*. Peabody, MA: Hendrickson, 1996.

Morgan, Christopher W. and Robert A. Peterson. *Heaven*. Wheaton, IL: Crossway, 2014.

Peterson, Robert A. *Salvation Accomplished by the Son: The Work of Christ*. Wheaton, IL: Crossway, 2012.

Plantinga Jr., Cornelius. *Not the Way It's Supposed to Be: A Breviary of Sin*. Grand Rapids, MI: Eerdmans, 1996.

Pratt, Richard L. *He Gave Us Stories: The Bible Student's Guide to Interpreting Old Testament Narratives*. Phillipsburg, NJ: P&R, 1993.

Richter, Sandra L. *The Epic of Eden: A Christian Entry into the Old Testament*. Downers Grove, IL: IVP Academic, 2008.

Ridderbos, Herman N. *Redemptive History and the New Testament Scriptures*, 2nd ed. Trans. by Richard B. Gaffin. Phillipsburg, NJ: P&R, 1988.

Sherman, Amy L. *Kingdom Calling: Vocational Stewardship for the Common Good.* Downers Grove, IL: InterVarsity, 2011.

Sklar, Jay. *Leviticus: An Introduction and Commentary.* Tyndale Old Testament Commentaries, Vol. 3. Downers Grove, IL: InterVarsity, 2014.

Vanhoozer, Kevin J. *The Drama of Doctrine: A Canonical-Linguistic Approach to Christian Theology.* Louisville, KY: Westminster John Knox Press, 2005.

Williams, Michael D. *Far as the Curse Is Found: The Covenant Story of Redemption.* Phillipsburg, NJ: P&R, 2005.

Wright, Christopher J.H. *Knowing Jesus Through the Old Testament.* Downers Grove, IL: InterVarsity, 1995.

——. *The Mission of God: Unlocking the Bible's Grand Narrative.* Downers Grove, IL: IVP Academic, 2006.

Wolters, Albert M. *Creation Regained: Biblical Basics for a Reformational Worldview.* 2nd ed. Grand Rapids, MI: Eerdmans, 2005.

NOTES

Your Invitation to Join the Greatest Drama of All Time

1. Herman Bavinck, *Reformed Dogmatics, Volume 1* (Grand Rapids, MI: Baker, 2008), 112.

Chapter 1

1. As stated by Michael D. Williams. This quote is to the best of my recollection.

2. Michael D. Williams, *Covenant Theology*, Covenant Theological Seminary, Fall 2010.

Chapter 2

1. Sandra L. Richter, *The Epic of Eden: A Christian Entry into the Old Testament* (Downers Grove, IL: IVP Academic, 2008), 103.

2. G.K. Beale and Mitchell Kim, *God Dwells Among Us: Expanding Eden to the Ends of the Earth* (Downers Grove, IL: InterVarsity, 2014), 30.

Chapter 3

1. Michael D. Williams, *Far as the Curse Is Found: The Covenant Story of Redemption* (Phillipsburg, NJ: P&R, 2005), 64.

2. Sandra L. Richter, *The Epic of Eden: A Christian Entry into the Old Testament* (Downers Grove, IL: IVP Academic, 2008), 104.

3. C. John Collins, *Did Adam and Eve Really Exist? Who They Were and Why You Should Care* (Wheaton, IL: Crossway, 2011), 55.

4. Keil and Delitzsch, *Commentary on the Old Testament* (Peabody, MA: Hendrickson Publishers, 2011), 67.

Chapter 4

1. Michael D. Williams, *Far as the Curse Is Found: The Covenant Story of Redemption* (Phillipsburg, NJ: P&R, 2005), xiv.

2. Williams, *Far as the Curse Is Found*, 88.

3. Williams, *Far as the Curse Is Found*, 114-15.

4. Williams, *Far as the Curse Is Found*, 95.

Chapter 5

1. Michael D. Williams, *Far as the Curse Is Found: The Covenant Story of Redemption* (Phillipsburg, NJ: P&R, 2005), 22.

2. Sandra L. Richter, *The Epic of Eden: A Christian Entry into the Old Testament* (Downers Grove, IL: IVP Academic, 2008), 174.

3. Williams, *Far as the Curse Is Found*, 34.

4. Kevin J. Vanhoozer, *The Drama of Doctrine: A Canonical-Linguistic Approach to Christian Theology* (Louisville, KY: Westminster John Knox Press, 2005), 386.

Chapter 6

1. T. Desmond Alexander, *From Eden to the New Jerusalem: An Introduction to Biblical Theology* (Grand Rapids, MI: Kregel Academic, 2009), 15.

2. Sandra L. Richter, *The Epic of Eden: A Christian Entry into the Old Testament* (Downers Grove, IL: IVP Academic, 2008), 182.

3. Jay Sklar, *Leviticus: An Introduction and Commentary*, Tyndale Old Testament Commentaries, Vol. 3 (Downers Grove, IL: InterVarsity Press, 2014), 37.

4. Michael D. Williams, *Far as the Curse Is Found: The Covenant Story of Redemption* (Phillipsburg, NJ: P&R, 2005), 180.

5. Richter, *The Epic of Eden*, 201

6. Christopher J.H. Wright, *Knowing Jesus Through the Old Testament* (Downers Grove, IL: IVP Academic, 2014), 24.

7. Richter, *The Epic of Eden*, 203

Chapter 7

1. Robert A. Peterson, *Salvation Accomplished by the Son: The Work of Christ* (Wheaton, IL: Crossway, 2012), 274.

2. Collins argues that the promise of Genesis 3:15 is a "promise of a specific human who will do battle with the evil power that spoke through the serpent, and at cost to himself will defeat the enemy, *for the sake of humans* (that is, not for himself)." C. John Collins, *Genesis 1-4: A Linguistic, Literary, and Theological Commentary* (Phillipsburg, NJ: P & R, 2006), 156.

3. Peterson, *Salvation*, 470

4. Peterson, *Salvation*, 472.

5. Fanny Crosby, "Redeemed, How I Love to Proclaim It!," 1882.

6. Jay Sklar, *Leviticus: An Introduction and Commentary*, Tyndale Old Testament Commentaries, Vol. 3 (Downers Grove, IL: InterVarsity Press, 2014), 27-28.

7. Cornelius Plantinga Jr., *Not the Way It's Supposed to Be: A Breviary of Sin* (Grand Rapids, MI: Wm. B. Eerdmans, 1996), 5.

8. These thoughts are taken from a sermon preached by Dr. Jay Sklar at Covenant Theological Seminary on April 28, 2011.

Chapter 8

1. Robert A. Peterson, *Salvation Accomplished by the Son: The Work of Christ* (Wheaton, IL: Crossway, 2012), 13.

2. Peterson, *Salvation Accomplished by the Son*, 64.

3. George Bennard, "The Old Rugged Cross," 1912.

4. Peterson, *Salvation Accomplished by the Son*, 152.

5. Sinclair B. Ferguson, *The Holy Spirit, Contours of Christian Theology* (Downers Grove, IL: InterVarsity, 1996), 57.

Chapter 9

1. Kevin J. Vanhoozer, *The Drama of Doctrine: A Canonical-Linguistic Approach to Christian Theology* (Louisville, KY: Westminster John Knox Press, 2005), 2-3.

2. Vanhoozer, *The Drama of Doctrine*, 2-3.

3. Alasdair MacIntyre, *After Virtue: A Study in Moral Theory*, 3rd ed. (University of Notre Dame Press, 2007), 213.

4. D.A. Carson and G.K. Beale, eds., *Commentary on the New Testament Use of the Old Testament* (Grand Rapids, MI: Baker Academic, 2007), 844, 846.

5. Amy L. Sherman, *Kingdom Calling: Vocational Stewardship for the Common Good* (Downers Grove, IL: InterVarsity, 2011), 23.

6. Christopher J.H. Wright, *The Mission of God: Unlocking the Bible's Grand Narrative* (Downers Grove, IL: IVP Academic, 2006), 200-01.

7. Wright, *The Mission of God*, 201.

8. Wright, *The Mission of God*, 213-14.

9. Wright, *The Mission of God*, 221.

10. Sandra L. Richter, *The Epic of Eden: A Christian Entry into the Old Testament* (Downers Grove,IL: IVP Academic, 2008), 222.

Chapter 10

1. Anthony A. Hoekema, *The Bible and the Future* (Grand Rapids, MI: Eerdmans, 1979), 280-281.

2. Michael D. Williams, *Far as the Curse Is Found: The Covenant Story of Redemption* (Phillipsburg, NJ: P&R, 2005), 281-288.

3. Albert Wolters, *Creation Regained: Biblical Basis for a Reformational Worldview* (Grand Rapids, MI: Eerdmans, 1985), 58.

4. Randy C. Alcorn, *Heaven* (Wheaton, IL: Tyndale, 2004), 88.

5. T. Desmond Alexander, *From Eden to the New Jerusalem: An Introduction to Biblical Theology* (Grand Rapids, MI: Kregel, 2009), 156.

6. Sandra L. Richter, *The Epic of Eden: A Christian Entry into the Old Testament* (Downers Grove, IL: IVP Academic, 2008), 182.

7. Richter, *The Epic of Eden*, 224.

8. Williams, *Far as the Curse Is Found*, 300-02.

To learn more about Harvest House books and
to read sample chapters, visit our website:

www.HarvestHousePublishers.com

HARVEST HOUSE PUBLISHERS
EUGENE, OREGON